T0017896

A 90-DAY DEVOTIONAL

PRAYER
WITH
PURPOSE
AND
POWER

DR. MYLES MUNROE

WHITAKER
HOUSE

Boldface type in Scripture quotations indicates the author's emphasis.

The forms LORD and GOD (in small capital letters) in Bible quotations represent the Hebrew name for God *Yahweh* (Jehovah), while *Lord* and *God* normally represent the name *Adonai*, in accordance with the Bible version used.

Prayer with Purpose and Power:
A 90-Day Devotional

Munroe Global • P.O. Box N9583 • Nassau, Bahamas
www.munroeglobal.com
office@munroeglobal.com

ISBN: 978-1-64123-949-3 • eBook ISBN: 978-1-64123-950-9
Printed in Colombia
© 2023 by Munroe Group of Companies Ltd.

Whitaker House • 1030 Hunt Valley Circle • New Kensington, PA 15068
www.whitakerhouse.com

Library of Congress Control Number: 2022948920

1 2 3 4 5 6 7 8 9 10 11   WH   30 29 28 27 26 25 24 23

CONTENTS

Part Two: Restored to Dominion Authority

Part Three: Entering into God's Presence

Part Four: Cultivating the God Kind of Faith

Part Five: Principles of Prayer

Part Eight: The Power of Prayer

INTRODUCTION

From his youth, Dr. Myles Munroe read and studied God's Word; and, for more than thirty years, he counseled and guided thousands of individuals to live lives of personal fulfillment and social and spiritual well-being. The knowledge and experience he gained led him to conclude that Christians can change the world if they truly understand the purpose and power of prayer, which God established in creation. It has always been God's purpose that we call heaven to earth.

As Dr. Munroe expressed,[1] "Prayer is meant to be one of the most exciting aspects of a life of faith. It has the power to transform lives, change circumstances, give peace and perseverance in the midst of trial, alter the course of nations, and win the world for Christ."

Yet he also stated, "I am convinced that prayer is one of the most misunderstood arts of the human experience. We avoid

---

1. The introduction and daily devotions in this book include edited excerpts from Myles Munroe, *Understanding the Purpose and Power of Prayer* (New Kensington, PA: Whitaker House, 2018).

prayer—both individually and corporately—because we don't understand it." Dr. Munroe recognized that Christians have many questions about aspects of prayer and that we face challenges in our practice of this vital art. "The greatest difficulty in most believers' experience is their prayer lives," he said. "Even though they believe prayer is a foundational element of the Christian life, they shy away from it because they don't really think it will make a difference. They don't pray because it hasn't seemed to work for them in the past, and they don't like failure.

"For many who do pray, the practice of prayer is merely a religious exercise, one that isn't concerned with obtaining results. Some believers have come to the conclusion—consciously or subconsciously—that prayer isn't very important to everyday life, that it doesn't apply to the real world. They look primarily to themselves or other people to meet their needs."

Dr. Munroe desired to demystify prayer for Christians so they could make use of what is rightfully theirs in Christ. "Prayer is not just an activity, a ritual, or an obligation. Nor is it begging God to do what we want Him to do. It is communion and communication with God that touches His heart. True prayer builds intimacy with God, honors His nature and character, respects His integrity, believes His Word, trusts in His love, affirms His purposes and will, and appropriates His promises."

Among the valuable prayer guidelines you will glean from these ninety devotionals are the "Twelve Action Steps in Prayer." Additionally, you will discover the tremendous effectiveness of employing the Word of God and calling on the name of Jesus as you intercede before your heavenly Father.

Also featured are daily Scripture readings. Since we discover the true purpose and power of prayer only in the mind of our Maker, it is essential to read His "Manual," as Dr. Munroe liked to call the Bible, for ourselves in order to clearly see the revelation of His plan for our lives. Whenever we study the Word of God, we should also pray and ask God for wisdom. The Holy Spirit is our Teacher, and we need to ask Him to illuminate the Word and give us insight.

Dr. Munroe wanted all believers to experience the life-changing power of prayer: "The power of prayer is the inheritance of the believer. It is God's desire that you experience intimacy with Him and spiritual strength to fulfill His purposes. I invite you to discover your power, authority, and rights in the earth and to position yourself to become a faith channel for heavenly influence in earth's affairs. Heaven depends on you, and earth needs you."

— Day 1 —

DOES PRAYER REALLY WORK?

"For the eyes of the Lord are on the righteous and his ears are attentive to their prayer." —1 Peter 3:12

Does God really hear me when I pray?" "Why does it seem as if my prayers just hit the ceiling and bounce back at me?" "Shouldn't I expect my prayers to be answered?"

Unanswered prayer is a major obstacle standing in the way of a life of true faith. Outwardly, we agree that prayer is worthwhile, but, secretly, we wonder what is wrong. We expect things to work if God said they are supposed to work.

When our prayers seem to go unanswered, what effect does this have on us? The spiritual and emotional pain can be deep and devastating:

+ *We feel abandoned by and isolated from God, imagining that He doesn't care about our problems.* We doubt His love for us, viewing Him as someone who is against us—or at least indifferent to us—instead of as a compassionate heavenly Father.

+ *We question God's character and integrity.* We may wonder, "Does God promise to answer my prayers or doesn't He?" We start to distrust Him.

+ *We feel as if our lives are unsettled and unstable.* We begin to rely on ourselves or on other people, groups, or beliefs, instead of on the power and promises of God, to meet our needs.

+ *We come to premature conclusions about ourselves and our prayers.* We may assume, "My prayers aren't answered because I don't have enough faith." Therefore, we don't come to understand the various truths and principles concerning prayer that God has given us in His Word.

• *We doubt our calling as God's intercessors.* We think, "Answered prayer must be only for an elite group of 'super-spiritual' Christians." In this way, we abandon a major purpose of God for our lives.

Frustration and confusion over unanswered prayer are understandable. I relate to the pain of unanswered prayer that you may be experiencing right now. I remember the many times I attended prayer meetings and, even while I was praying, wondered whether it was worth it or if prayer really worked at all. Sometimes, even as a Christian leader, I only went through the motions, with no belief in the very act of prayer I was participating in.

I've since come to recognize many of the obstacles that prevent prayer from being answered, as well as many principles of effective, powerful prayer. These principles are not obscure. They are readily available for you to begin practicing—today.

My approach is very practical; it is based on the clear teaching of the Word of God and over thirty years of experience in which I have, by God's grace, learned how to pray and receive answers to my prayers. Because I have learned and tested the truths of prayer, I also know the joy of its fulfillment. When you understand the biblical principles of the art of prayer, you will begin to communicate with God with power, grace, and confidence! You will enter into a new dimension of faith, deep love for God, and power for service.

⌒

Thought: When you understand the biblical principles of the art of prayer, you will begin to communicate with God with power, grace, and confidence!

Reading: Psalm 116:1–2

— DAY 2 —

THE PATHWAY TO ANSWERED PRAYER

"Call to me and I will answer you and tell you great and unsearchable things you do not know." —Jeremiah 33:3

Yesterday, we saw that when our prayers seem to go unanswered, the spiritual and emotional pain can be deep and devastating. It can undermine the foundation of our faith. It's like putting money into a soda machine that doesn't give a can of pop in return. You stand in front of it, becoming increasingly frustrated, until you finally kick it and walk away. You also never attempt to use it again. Many people have put in too many "prayer coins" and have received too few satisfying answers. Some Christians have been tempted to delve into ungodly activities because they were weary of not having their prayers answered. Others have lost their faith altogether because of unanswered prayer.

What is the pathway to answered prayer? The first step is to recognize the following truths:

First, God is faithful to answer prayer. Our understanding of prayer has become so distorted that we have developed a definition for the word that is the exact opposite of its true meaning. When we say something has no chance, or only a slight chance, of happening, we say, "It hasn't got a prayer." Yet Jesus gave us the assurance that God does hear and answer our prayers. He said, *"Therefore I tell you, whatever you ask for in prayer, believe that you have received it, and it will be yours"* (Mark 11:24). The answer is so sure that we are instructed to believe it has already happened.

This is not to say that the answers to our prayers will always manifest immediately. However, it does mean that every prayer based on the Word of God and offered in faith by a person who is in right relationship with God *is answered*—and that it is only a matter of time before that answer is evidenced. God answers as soon as we ask, and He reveals those answers in His timing. That is why Jesus told His disciples *"that they should always pray and not give up"* (Luke 18:1).

Second, when prayer does not bring results, it is an indication that something is wrong. God instituted prayer, and throughout the Old and New Testaments, there are numerous examples of prayers offered and answered. When prayer isn't answered, the Word of God generally provides an indication of why it was not answered, gives insight into the kind of prayers God responds to, and points out what can inhibit our prayers.

Third, God's will and Word **do** *work when they are understood and put into practice.* Whether you think so right now or not, prayer *does* work. However, it first needs to be understood. We must learn how to pray in a way that embodies the truths and principles of prayer that God has given us in His Word. The purpose of this devotional is to clearly set forth these truths and principles. Through them, you can begin today to change your outlook on God, yourself, and prayer. You can have an effective prayer life that will flow into all other areas of your life.

⌒

Thought: We must learn how to pray in a way that embodies the principles God has given us in His Word.

Reading: Matthew 7:7--8

GOD'S PURPOSE FOR PRAYER

"Then God said, 'Let us make man in our image, in our likeness, and let them rule....'"   —Genesis 1:26

To understand the purpose and principles of prayer, it is necessary to understand the mind and purpose of the Creator Himself. Prayer is a result of God's established authority structure between heaven and earth, as well as a product of His faithfulness to His Word. This is because prayer was born out of God's arrangements for mankind's assignment on earth. That assignment was established when the Creator spoke two words during the creation process: *"let them"*:

> Then God said, *"Let us make man in our image, in our likeness, and **let them** rule over the fish of the sea and the birds of the air, over the livestock, over all the earth, and over all the creatures that move along the ground."*   (Genesis 1:26)

These two words are critical for understanding the foundational principle of prayer because they define the *relationship* the Creator intended and desired with man and the planet earth.

How did God enable man to rule on earth? We know that He first created mankind out of His own essence, which is *spirit*. Yet since mankind needed to be able to rule in the *physical* realm of earth, God then gave humanity physical bodies manifested in two genders—male and female. This is why the Bible refers to the creation of man in both singular and plural terms: *"So God created man in his own image, in the image of God he created **him**; male and female he created **them**"* (Genesis 1:27). Thus, by "man," we are referring to mankind, both men and women, who were created to exercise dominion authority.[2]

---

2. To learn more about the distinct designs of the male and female and their dominion roles, please refer to the author's books *Understanding the Purpose and Power of Women* (2018) and *Understanding the Purpose and Power of Men* (2017), both published by Whitaker House.

The Creator's mandate for man to dominate the earth was established in the above declaration from Genesis 1:26, but, again, the parameters of that dominion were established by the words *"let them."* With these words, the Creator defined the boundaries of His right to legally influence and interfere in the earthly realm. This is based on the principle of God's integrity and His commitment to His word, which we will explore further in the next devotion.

Why is this so important? Because of the following four biblical principles, which will unfold for us as we progress in this devotional: (1) God's purpose is more important than our plans. (2) God has placed His word above even Himself. (3) God will never violate or break His word. (4) God's holiness is the foundation of His integrity and faithfulness.

These principles are essential to an understanding of the nature and purpose of prayer. It is these precepts that make prayer—our communication with our heavenly Father—necessary.

Let's look again at the first principle: *God's purpose is more important than our plans.* This principle establishes the truth that the Creator's commitment to His original intent for mankind is a priority for Him, and it motivates and regulates all His actions. In essence, everything God does is driven by His purposed desire, which never changes. His declaration is clear when He states, *"Many are the plans in a man's heart, but it is the LORD's purpose that prevails"* (Proverbs 19:21) and *"My purpose will stand, and I will do all that I please"* (Isaiah 46:10).

Thought: Everything God does is driven by His purposed desire, which never changes.

Reading: Isaiah 46:9–11

— DAY 4 —

CREATED TO REFLECT GOD'S NATURE

"The LORD Almighty has sworn, 'Surely, as I have planned, so it will be, and as I have purposed, so it will stand.'"
—Isaiah 14:24

The following Scripture, spoken by Jesus, as well as the verses about God's purpose that we reviewed in yesterday's devotion, reveal God's eternal, uncompromising commitment to His purpose and plans:

> *I tell you the truth, until heaven and earth disappear, not the smallest letter, not the least stroke of a pen, will by any means disappear from the Law until everything is accomplished.*
> (Matthew 5:18)

God's purpose is His will and intent, which He Himself will fulfill. He has spoken, *"My purpose will stand, and I will do all that I please"* (Isaiah 46:10).

Since God is a God of purpose, everything He created in this world, including men and women, has been designed to fulfill His purposes. God's actions are never arbitrary. Therefore, when God said, *"Let us make man in our image, in our likeness"* (Genesis 1:26), what does this statement reveal about His purpose for humanity?

The first revelation of His purpose for human beings is that *God created humanity to reflect His character and personality.* We were created to be like Him, having His *"image"* and *"likeness"* (Genesis 1:26). This means we were created to have His nature and moral character; they were meant to be the essence of our being.

The personal reason God created mankind was to establish a relationship of mutual love with humanity. God created mankind in His own image so love could be freely given and received between Creator and created. The only reason you and I can have fellowship with God is that God made us out of His own essence. He created us to be spirit, just as He is Spirit. *"God is spirit, and his worshipers must worship in spirit and in truth"* (John 4:24).

Although God is our Creator, He has always emphasized that He is our Father. It wasn't His desire to be primarily thought of as an awesome God or a *"consuming fire"* (Deuteronomy 4:24). God wants us to approach Him as children would a loving father: *"Is he not your Father, your Creator, who made you and formed you?"* (Deuteronomy 32:6). *"As a father has compassion on his children, so the LORD has compassion on those who fear him"* (Psalm 103:13).

Yet, although we were created out of God's essence, we are always dependent on God as our Source. As human beings, we are not self-sufficient, even though we would like to think we are! We cannot reveal God's image and likeness apart from a relationship with Him. We were intended to reflect God's nature in the context of being continually connected to Him in fellowship. First John 4:16 says, *"Whoever lives in love lives in God, and God in him."* You will never be truly satisfied with life until you love God. God must have the primary place in your life because you were designed to find fulfillment and ultimate meaning in Him.

⌒

Thought: God created mankind in His image, with His nature and moral character, and we are always meant to be dependent on Him as our Source.

Reading: Psalm 33:11

—Day 5—
CREATED TO HAVE DOMINION

"You made [human beings] *rulers over the works of your hands; you put everything under their feet."*
—Psalm 8:6 (NIV2011)

God's second purpose for human beings is that *He created humanity to have dominion over the world.* Remember that there is a twofold plan for mankind's dominion: one is *physical*, the other *spiritual.*

In the physical realm, God has entrusted the care of the earth to man. This means that we are to be the proprietors of the physical earth, including all the other living things in the world—fish, birds, livestock, all the animals. Adam was placed in the garden of Eden to tend and cultivate it. (See Genesis 2:15.) This is what mankind is to do with the entire earth: both tend it and cultivate it. God told humanity, in effect, "Rule over My world. Take care of it. Subdue it and fashion it with your own creativity." The earth is to be ruled over, taken care of, fashioned, and molded by beings made in the image of their Creator. We are meant to reflect the loving and creative Spirit of God.

This brings us to an interesting fact that many believers today often overlook: God didn't originally create man for heaven. He created man for the earth—for the garden. God is the Ruler of heaven, and He made man to express His authority in this world. God's plan for creation was this: as God ruled the unseen realm in heaven, man would rule the visible realm on earth, with God and man enjoying continual communion through their spiritual natures. God said, in effect, "I want what's happening in heaven to happen in the created world; I want My rule to extend to another realm, but I don't want to do it directly. I want man to share My rule."

Adam and Eve could fulfill this purpose only if they were relying on, and in constant communion with, the God of the garden. In the same way, we can function in the purposes for which we were created only as we are connected to our Source.

Yet having dominion means even more than taking care of the physical world. Since we are both physical and spiritual in nature, we are meant to carry out God's purposes for the earth not only in the physical realm but also in the spiritual realm. When God created Adam and Eve and placed them in the garden of Eden, it was never His intention that they leave the garden. Instead, He wanted the *garden to be spread over the entire earth.* What does this mean? God wanted them to take the character of the garden of Eden—God's presence, light, and truth—and spread it throughout the world. This is the overarching meaning of having dominion over the earth. Isaiah 11:9 says, *"The earth will be full of the knowledge of the LORD as the waters cover the sea."* This is still God's purpose today: for mankind to spread His presence, light, and truth throughout the earth. And one vital way in which we do this is through the relationship we have with God in prayer.

⌒

Thought: God wants us to take the character of the garden of Eden—God's presence, light, and truth—and spread it throughout the world.

Reading: Psalm 8:3–8

— Day 6 —

GOD UPHOLDS HIS WORD

"I will worship toward thy holy temple, and praise thy name for thy lovingkindness and for thy truth: for thou hast magnified thy word above all thy name."

—Psalm 138:2 (KJV)

To understand the purpose and power of prayer, we must also recognize that God's commitment to fulfill His purpose will never be at the expense of violating His spoken word or His written Word. Psalm 138:2 (KJV) tells us that He has placed His word even above His name.

It is God's commitment to His Word that is the basis of the prayer principle. The Word of God is not just the law for man, for it is also called "the Law of God." This implies that every word God speaks is also a law to Himself. He will subject Himself to His promises and decrees because of His integrity.

In the book of Psalms, we find these words:

Your word, O LORD, is eternal; it stands firm in the heavens. Your faithfulness continues through all generations.

(Psalm 119:89–90)

God is faithful to His Word at all costs. This being understood, we can appreciate the implications and impact of these initial words spoken by the Creator at man's creation: *"Let them rule* [*"have dominion"* KJV, NKJV] *over…the earth"* (Genesis 1:26).

Please note again that He did not say, "Let us" but rather, *"Let them."* With this statement, God created these seven primary laws:

1. The legal authority to dominate earth was given to mankind only.

2. God did not include Himself in the legal authority structure over the earth.

3. Man became the legal steward of the earthly domain.

4. Man is a spirit with a physical body; therefore, only spirits with physical bodies can legally function in the earthly realm.

5. Any spirit without a body is illegal on earth.

6. Any influence or interference from the supernatural realm on earth is legal only through mankind.

7. God, who is a Spirit without a physical body, made Himself subject to this law.

The following are the results of these laws, which were established by God Himself:

+ The legal authority on earth is in the hands of humankind.

+ The Creator, because of His integrity, will not violate the law of His Word.

+ Nothing will happen in the earthly realm without the active or passive permission of man, who is its legal authority.

+ The Creator and the heavenly beings cannot interfere in the earthly realm without the cooperation or permission of mankind.

+ God must obtain the agreement and cooperation of a person for whatever He desires to do in the earth.

As I will explain further in the next devotion, such a perspective may be a little shocking to some people. Yet these principles are critical for understanding the nature, power, and purpose of prayer. It is from these precepts that we will find the true definition of prayer.

⌒

Thought: The Creator, because of His integrity, will not violate the law of His Word.

Reading: Psalm 119:89–104

— Day 7 —

WHAT IS PRAYER?

*"Pray in the Spirit on all occasions with all kinds of prayers
and requests."* —Ephesians 6:18

What is the purpose of prayer?" "Doesn't God do whatever
He wants to do, anyway?" "Why should we have to pray when God
already knows everything, controls everything, predetermines
everything, and does not change?"

I believe these are valid questions, the answers to which we
began to explore in yesterday's devotion. We need to understand
essential truths about God's nature and His purposes for mankind
that lead to the necessity of prayer. That is why we began with the
biblical account of the creation of humanity to reveal these related
truths:

- Prayer is man giving God the legal right and permission to
  interfere in earth's affairs.

- Prayer is man giving heaven earthly license to influence earth.

- Prayer is a terrestrial license for celestial interference.

- Prayer is man exercising his legal authority on earth to invoke
  heaven's influence on the planet.

Again, these definitive aspects of prayer may be a little shocking to some, but a closer study will help explain many scriptural
statements as they relate to heavenly activities on earth. Let's take
a look at a few of those statements:

*If my people, who are called by my name, will humble them-
selves and pray and seek my face and turn from their wicked
ways, then will I hear from heaven and will forgive their sin
and will heal their land.* (2 Chronicles 7:14)

Then Jesus told his disciples a parable to show them that they should always pray and not give up. (Luke 18:1)

And pray in the Spirit on all occasions with all kinds of prayers and requests. With this in mind, be alert and always keep on praying for all the saints. (Ephesians 6:18)

Be joyful always; pray continually ["without ceasing" KJV, NKJV]; give thanks in all circumstances, for this is God's will for you in Christ Jesus. (1 Thessalonians 5:16–18)

Clearly, God desires His people to communicate with Him through prayer. Every action taken by God on the earth has required the involvement of a human being. To rescue humanity in the flood, He needed Noah. For the creation of a nation, He needed Abraham. To lead the nation of Israel, He needed Moses. To bring back Israel from captivity, He needed Daniel. To defeat Jericho, He needed Joshua. For the preservation of the Hebrews, He needed Esther. For the salvation of mankind, *He needed to become a man.*

Prayer is therefore not optional for mankind but a necessity. If we don't pray, heaven cannot intervene in earth's affairs. It is imperative that we take responsibility for the earth and determine what happens here by our prayer lives.

As John Wesley once said, "God does nothing but in answer to prayer."[3]

Thought: Every action taken by God on the earth has required the involvement of a human being.

Reading: 2 Chronicles 7:14–15

---

3. John Wesley, in E. M. Bounds, *Power through Prayer* (New Kensington, PA: Whitaker House, 2012), 117.

PRAYER IS FELLOWSHIP WITH GOD

"I will walk among you and be your God, and you will be my people."   —Leviticus 26:12

Who prayed the first prayer? I would say that it was Adam because he was created first and God spoke to him first concerning how to tend the garden and about the parameters of mankind's dominion on earth. (See Genesis 2:15–17.) The Bible implies that God made a practice of walking and talking with Adam in the cool of the day. (See Genesis 3:8–9.) The fellowship between God and Adam, and Adam's agreement with God's purposes, formed the essence of the first prayer. You may say, "Yes, but Adam was already in the presence of God. Why did he need to pray?"

Adam needed to pray because, from creation, prayer was to be a place of purity before God in which we reflect His nature and a oneness with His purposes, in which our wills are in total agreement with His will. The heart of prayer is communion with God in a unity of love and purpose. It is also our agreeing with God—heart, soul, mind, and strength—to bring about God's will on the earth.

The account of the creation of mankind shows us that God never desired or intended to rule the earth by Himself. Why? It is because *"God is love"* (1 John 4:8, 16), and love doesn't think in those terms. A selfish person wants all the glory, all the credit, all the power, all the authority, all the rights, and all the privileges. But a person of love wants others to share in what he has. It is crucial for us to understand that the *relationship of love* that God established with mankind is not separate from the *purpose* God has for mankind. Rather, the relationship is foundational to the purpose; both are vital keys to prayer.

The essence of prayer is therefore twofold:

1. Prayer is an expression of mankind's unity and *relationship* of love with God, our Father.

2. Prayer is an expression of mankind's affirmation of and participation in God's *purposes* for the earth.

Again, to fully understand the essence of prayer, we need to recognize that prayer began with the *creation* of mankind. It was not instituted *after* Adam and Eve's fall but *before* it. Prayer existed from the beginning of God's relationship with human beings. To pray means to commune with God, to become one with Him. It means union with God—unity and singleness of purpose, thought, desire, will, reason, motive, objective, and feelings. H. D. Bollinger said, "Prayer is being expressing relationship with being."

Prayer is man's vehicle of the soul and spirit by which he communes with the invisible God. It is also the medium through which the human spirit affects and is affected by the will and purpose of the divine Creator. Therefore, we can say the following:

Prayer is the involvement of oneself (one's whole self) with God.

⌣⁀

Thought: God desired offspring with whom He could share a relationship of love, as well as rulership and dominion.

Reading: 1 John 1:3

— Day 9 —

PRAYER IS EXERCISING DOMINION

"This is the confidence we have in approaching God: that if we ask anything according to his will, he hears us."

—1 John 5:14

Prayer is necessary for God's will to be done in the earth.

God causes things to happen on earth when men and women pray in agreement with His will. As we are learning, our need to pray is a result of the way God arranged dominion and authority for the earth: God created the world. Then He made men and women and gave them dominion over all the works of His hands. Since God never breaks His word concerning how things are to work, prayer is mandatory, not optional, for spiritual progress and victory in our individual lives and in the world at large. God moves in answer to prayer.

God's plan for man's dominion authority is for us to desire what He desires, to will what He wills, and to ask Him to accomplish His purposes in the world so that goodness and truth may reign on the earth rather than evil and darkness. In this sense, prayer is man giving God the freedom to intervene in earth's affairs.

As a member of the human race, created in the image of God, you have this dominion authority as your heritage. God's desire is for you to will *His* will. His will is meant to be the backbone and center of your prayers, the heart of your intercession, the source of your confidence in supplication, the strength of your fervent and effectual prayers.

Praying does not mean convincing God to do *your* will but doing *His* will through your will. Jesus's assurance in prayer was based on His knowing and doing God's will. As it says in 1 John 5:

This is the confidence we have in approaching God: that if we ask anything according to his will, he hears us. And if we know that he hears us—whatever we ask—we know that we have what we asked of him.   (1 John 5:14–15)

Therefore, the key to effective prayer is understanding God's purpose for your life, His reason for your existence—as a human being in general and as an individual specifically.[4] This is an especially important truth to remember: once you understand your purpose, it becomes the "raw material," the foundational matter, for your prayer life. God's will is the authority of your prayers. Prayer is calling forth what God has already purposed and predestined, continuing His work of creation and the establishment of His plans for the earth.

In this way, your purpose in God is the foundational material for your prayers regarding...

provision	endurance	thanksgiving
healing	patience	confidence
deliverance	authority	assurance
power	faith	boldness
protection	praise	peace

...for the supply of *all* your needs. Everything you need is available to fulfill your purpose. All that God is, and all that He has, may be received through prayer.

⌒

Thought: God's will is His purpose for mankind. To fulfill what we were created to be and do, we must desire to do God's will.

Reading: Psalm 40:8

---

4. The focus of this devotional is on God's overall purposes for humanity and how they are fulfilled through prayer. For more teaching on finding one's individual purpose, please see the following books on vision by Dr. Myles Munroe: *The Principles and Power of Vision* (New Kensington, PA: Whitaker House, 2003) and *Vision with Purpose and Power: A 90-Day Devotional* (New Kensington, PA: Whitaker House, 2022).

PRAYER IS ASKING GOD TO INTERVENE IN HUMAN AFFAIRS

"If we know that he hears us—whatever we ask—we know that we have what we asked of him." —1 John 5:15

Wwhen we know God's will, when we are obedient to it, and when we ask God to fulfill it, God will grant what we ask of Him. Whether we are praying for individual, family, community, national, or world needs, we must seek to be in agreement with God's will so that His purposes can reign in the earth. This is the essence of exercising dominion.

When we pray, we carry out our responsibility to demonstrate what our relationship with God means in terms of living and ruling in the world. As we have seen, because God gave humanity authority over the earth at creation, He requires the permission or authorization of mankind in order to act on the earth. This is why it is so vital that we pray. When we stop praying, we allow God's purposes for the world to be hindered. Recall that Jesus taught His disciples *"that they should always pray and not give up"* (Luke 18:1). He also said, *"I will give you the keys of the kingdom of heaven; whatever you bind on earth will be bound in heaven, and whatever you loose on earth will be loosed in heaven"* (Matthew 16:19).

Knowing these truths is necessary for effective prayer. We need to ask God to intervene in human affairs. If we don't, our world will be susceptible to the influences of Satan and sin. God will ultimately bring His purposes to pass in the world—with or without our individual cooperation. If you do not pray, He will eventually find someone who will agree with His plans. However, when you neglect to pray, you are failing to fulfill *your* role in His purposes. He does not want you to miss out on this privilege—for your sake, as well as His. James 4:2 says, *"You do not have, because you do not ask God."*

Once more, prayer is not optional for the believer. It is a necessity in order to fulfill God's purposes in the world and in our individual lives. Time spent in prayer is not time wasted but time invested. As we embrace the will of God, as we live before Him in the righteousness of Christ, as we seek to fulfill His purposes, nothing will be able to hinder our prayers, and we will begin to understand Jesus's saying in Matthew 19:26, *"With God all things are possible."*

Thought: Prayer is not optional. It is a necessity in order to fulfill God's purposes in the world and in our individual lives.

Reading: Psalm 145:17–19

— Day 11 —

"I WILL ANSWER HIM"

"He will call upon me, and I will answer him; I will be with him in trouble, I will deliver him and honor him."
—Psalm 91:15

Prayer is meant to be answered—or else God would not ask us to pray. He isn't interested in wasting your time and efforts. He is too practical for that. He is interested in results, not just *"many words"* (Matthew 6:7) spoken in prayer. Jesus's approach to prayer was also very practical. He didn't pray without expecting to be heard. At one point, He said, *"Father, I thank you that you have heard me. I knew that you **always** hear me, but I said this for the benefit of the people standing here, that they may believe that you sent me"* (John 11:41–42). We need to know how to approach God and to learn the kind of prayers God responds to. We need to pray as Jesus prayed.

God is loving and gracious. He knows we have a limited understanding of Himself and His ways, and that we struggle with our fallen nature. That is why He will, at times, answer our prayers even when they are weak and full of doubt. However, as a loving Father, He wants us to grow and mature. He doesn't want to leave us in our weakness and uncertainty. He wants us to enter into His purposes because that is where we can truly be children of our heavenly Father, work together with Him, and live the abundant life Christ came to give us. (See John 10:10.) Therefore, at times, He will withhold answers to prayer so we will seek Him and the principles of prayer that are essential for praying according to His will and for appropriating His promises and power.

True prayer will do the following:

- build intimacy with God
- bring honor to His nature and character
- produce respect for His integrity
- enable belief in His Word
- cause trust in His love
- affirm His purposes and will
- appropriate His promises

As we prepare to learn more about prayer with purpose and power in the coming days, let's pray together:

Heavenly Father,

You have said, *"Call to me and I will answer you and tell you great and unsearchable things you do not know"* (Jeremiah 33:3). On the basis of this promise, we call to You and ask You to show us great and unsearchable truths about prayer that You have set forth in Your Word. Give us open minds and hearts to hear Your Word and to allow the Holy Spirit to teach us Your purposes and truth. We pray this in the name of Jesus, our Wisdom and our Strength. Amen.

Thought: Prayer is meant to be answered—or else God would not ask us to pray.

Reading: Psalm 32:6–7

— DAY 12 —

BROKEN RELATIONSHIP, BROKEN EFFECTIVENESS IN PRAYER

"Sin entered the world through one man, and death through sin, and in this way death came to all people, because all sinned."　　　　　　　　—Romans 5:12 (NIV2011)

God gave humanity a vast amount of freedom and authority on earth. Yet these gifts were dependent on man's using his will to do the will of God. If he used his will for anything other than God's will, the image and likeness of God within him would be marred, and the purposes of God for the world would be obstructed—purposes of goodness, fruitfulness, creativity, truth, joy, and love. The rebellion of Adam and Eve brought about this distortion of God's image in mankind and thus attacked God's plans for the earth. This happened because man used his will for *self-serving* purposes, while God's will is based on *His love.*

How did this rebellion come about? Satan tempted Adam and Eve to disobey God, and they chose to agree with Satan's purposes rather than with God's. In doing so, human beings sinned and cut off communion with God. Humanity no longer agreed with the Creator to fulfill His purposes for earth—leaving the world at the mercy of a renegade authority. When man forfeited his authority to Satan, a new ruler was introduced on earth—one bent on its destruction rather than its growth in godliness and fruitfulness. Because Satan usurped mankind's authority on earth, the apostle Paul referred to him as *"the god of this world"* (2 Corinthians 4:4 KJV).

When Adam and Eve broke their relationship with God, *their effectiveness in prayer was also broken.* Remember, true prayer is maintained through oneness of heart and purpose with God.

Only then can we fulfill God's ways and plans. When we pray, we represent God's interests on earth, and representation requires relationship. Therefore, our difficulties with prayer can be traced directly to the fall and the resulting fallen nature of man, through which we were estranged from God.

If we are to be restored to God's purposes in the crucial area of prayer, we must realize and act upon who we are in Christ and the principles of prayer that God has established. We may not think of prayer as being an area in which we need to be *"transformed by the renewing of* [our] *mind"* (Romans 12:2). However, since effective prayer has *everything* to do with being united with God in a relationship of love, having a heart and mind in union with God's will, gaining a discerning mind regarding His purposes, and exercising faith in His Word, it is a vital area in which we need to be transformed.

> *Do not conform any longer to the pattern of this world, but be transformed by the renewing of your mind. Then you will be able to test and approve what God's will is—his good, pleasing and perfect will.* (Romans 12:2)

Thought: When Adam and Eve broke their relationship with God, their effectiveness in prayer was also broken.

Reading: Romans 5:10–15

WHAT GIVES US THE RIGHT TO PRAY?

"We have confidence to enter the Most Holy Place by the blood of Jesus." —Hebrews 10:19

Earlier in this devotional, we asked the question "What is the *purpose* of prayer?" We essentially defined the twofold purpose of prayer that was established at creation in this way: (1) Prayer is the vehicle by which you are meant to commune with the invisible God. (2) Prayer is the medium through which your spirit is intended to affect and be affected by the will and purpose of the divine Creator.

That's the *purpose* of prayer. However, on what basis do you have a *right* to go before God in prayer? You must be certain of the answer to this question in your own heart and mind if you are to have an effective prayer life.

Originally, God gave us the right to pray by virtue of our relationship with Him and our purpose of exercising dominion over the earth. Yet our relationship with our Creator was broken through the sin of our first ancestors, and our dominion authority was forfeited. At that point, Satan, rather than man, became *"the god of this world"* (2 Corinthians 4:4 KJV). Where did this leave people in relation to communion with God and His purposes for prayer? They became estranged from Him and His plans for them, so that they...

+ felt isolated from God.

+ were unsure of where they stood with Him.

+ didn't know what God wanted to do for and through them.

+ lost their sense of purpose.

Do these results sound at all like your own prayer life? If so, you must realize that your concept of prayer has been influenced by the effects of the fall. However, God wants to give you a new outlook on prayer, one that reflects His purposes for redemption as well as creation. One that reaffirms your right to pray.

How could God enable humanity to regain a relationship with Him and authority on the earth when man had thrown away these gifts by his own choice? We need to appreciate the magnitude of man's dilemma. Man's sin would have to be dealt with. Man would also have to want to return to God and work together with Him of his own free will. These were no simple matters. Restoring mankind would have been impossible if it were not for Jesus Christ. As Jesus Himself said, *"With man this is impossible, but with God all things are possible"* (Matthew 19:26). God's eternal plan for humanity was made possible through the coming of Jesus Christ.

Only through Christ are we restored to our purposes in God.

Only through Christ do we have a right to pray to God with dominion authority.

⟲

Thought: God wants to give you a new outlook on prayer, one that reflects His purposes for redemption as well as creation.

Reading: Hebrews 10:19–22

— Day 14 —

JESUS RESTORED OUR AUTHORITY

*"In [Jesus] and through faith in him we may approach God
with freedom and confidence."* —Ephesians 3:12

From the beginning, God planned for man's redemption and
restoration of purpose to come through Jesus Christ.

> [God] *made known to us the mystery of his will according to
> his good pleasure, which he purposed in Christ…. His intent
> was that now, through the church, the manifold wisdom of
> God should be made known to the rulers and authorities in
> the heavenly realms, according to his eternal purpose which he
> accomplished in Christ Jesus our Lord. In him and through
> faith in him we may approach God with freedom and confi-
> dence.* (Ephesians 1:9; 3:10–12)

How could Christ accomplish God's *"eternal purpose"*? To
restore God's purpose, Jesus had to come as a Representative of
the legal authority of the earth—man. He had to come as a *human
being*, as the Second Adam, as the beginning of a new family of
mankind who would be devoted to God—*"the firstborn among
many brothers"* (Romans 8:29). Scripture says, *"The Word became
flesh and made his dwelling among us"* (John 1:14). If He had not
come as a man, He would not have had the right to reclaim humanity and the earth for God, according to the way God has ordered
His purposes for the world.

Also, to restore man's broken relationship with God, Jesus had
to be without sin, and He had to *choose* to do the will of God.
Only a perfectly righteous man who desired to do God's will could
redeem humanity. The Bible says, *"God made him who had no sin to*

be sin for us, so that in him we might become the righteousness of God" (2 Corinthians 5:21). Therefore, the second person of the Trinity voluntarily put aside His heavenly glory and came to earth as a man:

> [Christ], *being in very nature God, did not consider equality with God something to be grasped, but made himself nothing, taking the very nature of a servant, being made in human likeness. And being found in appearance as a man, he humbled himself and became obedient to death—even death on a cross!* (Philippians 2:6–8)

God gave mankind the freedom to function as the legal authority on earth. He placed His will for the earth on the cooperation of man's will. This purpose never changed, even after the fall of mankind.

It is essential for us to remember these truths:

+ Jesus came as a man. Thus, He was qualified as a Representative of earthly authority.

+ Jesus was perfectly obedient and sinless. Thus, He was qualified to be the Son of God and to restore man's relationship with the Father by overcoming sin and death through His sacrifice on the cross.

+ Jesus rose victoriously. Thus, He was qualified to defeat sin and Satan, regain authority over the earth, be the earth's rightful King, and reestablish man's God-given authority for dominion.

⌒

Thought: To restore God's purpose, Jesus had to come as a Representative of the legal authority of the earth—man.

Reading: Romans 5:17–19

JESUS IS THE SECOND ADAM

"It is written: 'The first man Adam became a living being'; the last [second] Adam, a lifegiving spirit."

—1 Corinthians 15:45

Christ accomplished our redemption and reclaimed our earthly authority by being the Second Adam. *"For as in Adam all die, so in Christ all will be made alive"* (1 Corinthians 15:22).

Here are three qualities Christ manifests as the Second Adam:

1. *Jesus is the image of God.* Jesus reflects God's image, just as Adam had originally done. Jesus is called *"Christ, who is the image of God"* (2 Corinthians 4:4). Also, as the second person of the Trinity, Jesus retained His divinity, so that Christ is both fully human and fully God. This means that the fullness of the *"image of God"* was revealed in both His humanity and His divinity: *"God was pleased to have all his fullness dwell in him"* (Colossians 1:19). *"For in Christ all the fullness of the Deity lives in bodily form, and you have been given fullness in Christ, who is the head over every power and authority"* (Colossians 2:9–10). *"He is the image of the invisible God, the firstborn over all creation"* (Colossians 1:15).

2. *Jesus has a unique and deep relationship of love with God,* perfectly reflecting the relationship God desired to have with Adam and Eve.

> *The Father loves the Son and has placed everything in his hands.* (John 3:35)

> *For the Father loves the Son and shows him all he does.* (John 5:20)

The love of the Father and the Son is so deep and reciprocal that Jesus could say, "*I and the Father are one*" (John 10:30).

3. *Jesus lives to do God's will.* The above verses remind us of the connection between love for God and oneness with His purposes, which was characteristic of humanity's original relationship with God. Throughout the Gospels, Jesus revealed that His one purpose and objective in life was to do the will of God:

> "*My food,*" said Jesus, "*is to do the will of him who sent me and to finish his work.*" (John 4:34)

> *I can of Myself do nothing. As I hear, I judge; and My judgment is righteous, because I do not seek My own will but the will of the Father who sent Me.* (John 5:30 NKJV)

> *For I have come down from heaven not to do my will but to do the will of him who sent me.* (John 6:38)

Jesus lives to do the will of God. He is one with God and His purposes, and He said that anyone who does God's will belongs to the family of God: "*Whoever does the will of my Father in heaven is my brother and sister and mother*" (Matthew 12:50).

⌒

Thought: Jesus has a unique and deep relationship of love with God, perfectly reflecting the relationship God desired to have with Adam and Eve.

Reading: Matthew 26:39, 42

—Day 16—
JESUS REIGNS WITH AUTHORITY

"Then Jesus came to them and said, 'All authority in heaven and on earth has been given to me.'"   —Matthew 28:18

Just as Adam and Eve were meant to administer God's rule on earth, Christ exhibited the authority of God while He lived on earth: *"The blind receive sight, the lame walk, those who have leprosy are cured, the deaf hear, the dead are raised, and the good news is preached to the poor"* (Matthew 11:5). His authority and reign were powerfully manifested when He rose from the dead and conquered sin, Satan, and death. When Jesus returns to earth, His authority will be recognized by the whole world:

> *...that at the name of Jesus every knee should bow, in heaven and on earth and under the earth, and every tongue confess that Jesus Christ is Lord, to the glory of God the Father.*
> (Philippians 2:10–11)

> *On his robe and on his thigh he has this name written: KING OF KINGS AND LORD OF LORDS.*   (Revelation 19:16)

> *The kingdom of the world has become the kingdom of our Lord and of his Christ, and he will reign for ever and ever.*
> (Revelation 11:15)

Because He was the perfect Man and the perfect Sacrifice, Jesus has the right and the power to reign on the earth and to ask God to intervene in the world. This means that even if no other people are in agreement with God, God's purposes for the earth can be brought about in Christ. His prayers for mankind are powerful and effective. *"Therefore he is able to save completely those who* come to God through him, because he always lives to intercede for them" (Hebrews 7:25).

In addition, Jesus has given believers His Spirit so that we can agree with God's purposes even when we are uncertain about how to pray. *"In the same way, the Spirit helps us in our weakness. We do not know what we ought to pray for, but the Spirit himself intercedes for us with groans that words cannot express"* (Romans 8:26).

Prayer is both a right and a privilege of redeemed man. I cannot emphasize enough the vital relationship between redemption and true prayer.

The position and authority that Jesus won have been *transferred back to us* through spiritual rebirth in Christ. (See John 3:5.) When we believe in and receive Jesus Christ, our relationship with God and our authority on earth are restored! Because of Christ, we can live again as true sons and daughters of God, with all the rights and privileges associated with being His offspring. We can rejoice that now we are in our rightful position to enter fully into a relationship of love with God and to agree that "His kingdom come, His will be done on earth as it is in heaven." (See Matthew 6:10.)

It is God's will that every person be redeemed and rule the earth through the Spirit of Christ. It is through mankind that God desires to reveal His character, nature, principles, precepts, and righteousness to the visible world. This is God's *eternal* plan. It applies to our present lives on earth, and it will apply throughout eternity.

~

Thought: The position and authority that Jesus won have been transferred back to us through spiritual rebirth in Christ.

Reading: Ephesians 1:19–23

—DAY 17—

WHO ARE WE IN CHRIST?

"For you know that it was not with perishable things such as silver or gold that you were redeemed from the empty way of life handed down to you from your forefathers, but with the precious blood of Christ, a lamb without blemish or defect."

—1 Peter 1:18–19

Who are we in Christ?

We are new creations. The Scripture says, *"If anyone is in Christ, he is a new creation; the old has gone, the new has come! All this is from God"* (2 Corinthians 5:17–18). This is not something we have made up. It is not presumption on our part. It is from God. Therefore, we don't have to be afraid to say it and to live in its wonderful reality.

We are the redeemed. This is not just a philosophy or an opinion. This is the Father's description of who we are in His Son. The Second Adam redeemed mankind. As a result, not only are we new creations, but we also have a redemption that is literal and absolute. Our redemption restores our dominion.

What does this redemption mean to us?

1. *Satan has no authority over us.* Satan is the prince of darkness, and he became the god of this world when he successfully tempted Adam and Eve to reject God's ways. Yet, through Christ, we have been delivered from Satan's dominion, out of the realm of darkness. That is why, even though we continue to live in a fallen world, we do not belong to it. We belong to God's kingdom: *"He has rescued us from the dominion of darkness and brought us into the kingdom of the Son he loves"* (Colossians 1:13). *"But you are a chosen people, a royal priesthood, a holy nation, a people belonging to God,*

that you may declare the praises of him who called you out of darkness into his wonderful light" (1 Peter 2:9). Because we have been delivered from Satan's dominion, the enemy no longer has authority over us. Rather, we have authority over him in the name of Jesus.

2. *Sin has no authority over us.* Christ has also delivered us from the dominion and power of sin. *"Sin shall not be your master, because you are not under law, but under grace"* (Romans 6:14). The Bible says that when we have repented of our sins and believed in Jesus as our Substitute and Representative, we are *"in Christ"* (2 Corinthians 5:17). We are *"the righteousness of God"* in Him (verse 21). Since He is sinless, we, also, are free from sin. We may not always appreciate or appropriate this fact, but it is still true. *"Where sin increased, grace increased all the more, so that, just as sin reigned in death, so also grace might reign through righteousness to bring eternal life through Jesus Christ our Lord"* (Romans 5:20–21). Therefore, because of redemption, sin no longer reigns in our lives—grace does.

Thought: Man's redemption allows him to have dominion.

Reading: 1 Peter 1:18–21

— Day 18 —

AUTHORITY IN JESUS'S NAME AND WORD

"If you remain in me and my words remain in you, ask whatever you wish, and it will be given you." —John 15:7

Our redemption has also given us authority in Jesus's name and in His Word. Jesus clearly stated:

I tell you the truth, anyone who has faith in me will do what I have been doing. He will do even greater things than these, because I am going to the Father. And I will do whatever you ask in my name, so that the Son may bring glory to the Father. You may ask me for anything in my name, and I will do it.
(John 14:12–14)

The authority of Jesus's name gives us access to our heavenly Father. Our right to *"approach the throne of grace with confidence"* (Hebrews 4:16) brings us the delight of a restored relationship with God. This essential aspect of prayer also enables us to agree with the Father and His purposes, and to ask Him to fulfill His Word as He meets our needs and the needs of others.

In that day you will ask in my name. I am not saying that I will ask the Father on your behalf. No, the Father himself loves you because you have loved me and have believed that I came from God.
(John 16:26–27)

God's presence, power, and unlimited resources are available to us in the name of Jesus. Yet Jesus's name isn't a magic word we use to get what we want. We must pray according to God's will, which we find in His Word. Jesus said in John 15:7, *"If you remain in me and my words remain in you, ask whatever you wish, and it will be given you."* The backbone of prayer is our agreement with God's Word, our oneness with Christ, who is the Living Word, and our unity with God's purposes and will.

Power in prayer is not based on emotions, feelings, or the theories of men but upon the Word of God, *"which lives and abides forever"* (1 Peter 1:23 NKJV). God's Word is the guarantee of answered prayer. God is asking you to bring Him His Word, to plead your covenantal rights. We are not to pray to God in ignorance but as partners in His purposes.

Prayer is joining forces with God the Father by calling attention to His promises. *"No matter how many promises God has made, they are 'Yes' in Christ. And so through him the 'Amen' is spoken by us to the glory of God"* (2 Corinthians 1:20). The *New King James Version* expresses it in this way: *"For all the promises of God in Him are Yes, and in Him Amen, to the glory of God through us."*

⌒

Thought: Prayer is joining forces with God the Father by calling attention to His promises.

Reading: 2 Peter 3:9

JESUS IS OUR MODEL OF AUTHORITY

*"I tell you the truth, the Son can do nothing by himself; he can
do only what he sees his Father doing."*   —John 5:19

Jesus is not only the One who reclaimed our dominion authority,
but He is also our model for how we are to live in this authority.
He is what we are to be. His prayer life is an example of the prayer
life we are to have.

You may say, "Yes, but Jesus was different from us when He
walked on the earth. He was divine, and so He had an advantage
over us."

When Jesus was on earth, was He in a better position than
we are? No. What He accomplished on earth, He accomplished
in His humanity, not His divinity. Otherwise, He could not have
been man's Representative and Substitute. As the Son of Man,
Jesus kept a close relationship with the Father through prayer. He
did what God directed Him to do and what He saw God actively
working to accomplish in the world. He relied on the grace and
Spirit of God. We can do the same. Jesus said:

> *My Father is always at his work to this very day, and I, too,
> am working.... I tell you the truth, the Son can do nothing by
> himself; he can do only what he sees his Father doing, because
> whatever the Father does the Son also does. For the Father
> loves the Son and shows him all he does. (John 5:17, 19–20)*

God loved Jesus because He was perfectly obedient and lived
to fulfill God's purposes. "*The reason my Father loves me is that I lay
down my life—only to take it up again*" (John 10:17). God revealed
to Jesus what He was doing in the world and how Jesus's ministry

related to His overall purpose. I believe that God will do the same for us as we live and work in the Spirit of Christ.

> *The words I say to you are not just my own. Rather, it is the Father, living in me, who is doing his work. Believe me when I say that I am in the Father and the Father is in me.*
> (John 14:10–11)

Jesus's prayers were effective because He had a relationship with God, knew His purposes, and prayed according to God's will—according to what God had already spoken and promised to do. We are to imitate Him. More than that, we are to let His Spirit and attitude rule in our lives. *"Let this mind be in you which was also in Christ Jesus"* (Philippians 2:5 NKJV). We are to live in the new covenant that God has granted us in Christ, which restores us to oneness with God's heart and will: *"'This is the covenant I will make with the house of Israel after that time,' declares the LORD. 'I will put my law in their minds and write it on their hearts. I will be their God, and they will be my people'"* (Jeremiah 31:33).

⌣

Thought: Jesus's prayers were effective because He had a relationship with God, knew His purposes, and prayed according to God's will.

Reading: John 14:10–14

— DAY 20 —

ARE YOU WILLING?

"Who is he who will devote himself to be close to me?"
—Jeremiah 30:21

Several days ago, I asked you to consider what gives you the *right* to pray. God's Word gave us the answer: it is not only your *initial calling in creation* but also your *redemption in Christ* that gives you this right. This is a solid and life-changing truth! It takes away doubt, fear, uncertainty, and timidity regarding your prayer life.

Because of Christ, you no longer have to feel isolated from God or unsure of where you stand with Him and His purposes. Instead, you can have a relationship of love with God your Father, the certainty of your redemption in Christ, an understanding of your calling and authority in Christ, and a clear idea of God's purpose for your life. God wants you to live confidently in the authority He has given you.

Do you want God to bring about His purposes for your life and for our fallen world? You can invite Him to do so through prayer.

From Genesis to Revelation, God always found a human being to help Him accomplish His purposes. He comes to you now and asks, in effect, "Are you willing? Will you help Me fulfill My purposes for your life and for the earth? Or are you content to live an unfulfilled existence and to let the influences of sin and Satan encroach upon our world? *'Who is he who will devote himself to be close to me?'"* (See Jeremiah 30:21.)

If you are willing to devote yourself to becoming closer to God, then begin today to apply the redemption of Christ to your prayer life by acknowledging Jesus's restoration of your relationship with the Father and your purpose of dominion.

Remind yourself daily that your redemption means Satan and sin no longer have authority over you, that you have authority and access to the Father through Jesus's name, and that you have authority through the Word of God.

I pray that you will desire to draw closer to God, to live in oneness with Him and His purposes, and to exercise the dominion authority He has given you through the Spirit of Christ. Let's pray:

Heavenly Father,

You have said, *"Many are the plans in a man's heart, but it is the LORD's purpose that prevails"* (Proverbs 19:21). We ask You to fulfill Your Word and make Your purpose reign in our lives. We all have plans and goals that we are pursuing. We ask You to establish whatever is from You—whatever is in line with Your purpose—and cause to fade away whatever is not from You. We honor You as our Creator and as our loving heavenly Father. We affirm that it is You who works in us to will and to act according to Your good purpose, as it says in Philippians 2:13. Renew our minds so we may understand Your ways and Your plans more fully. We pray this in the name of Jesus, who is our Way, Truth, and Life. Amen.

⌒

Thought: The foundation of prayer is our agreement with God's Word, our oneness in Christ, who is the Living Word, and our unity with God's purposes and will.

Reading: Matthew 18:18–19

—DAY 21—

HOW DO WE BEGIN TO PRAY?

"Who may ascend the hill of the LORD? Who may stand in his holy place? He who has clean hands and a pure heart."
—Psalm 24:3–4

How do we begin to pray? Where do we start? Since the heart of prayer is communion with God in a unity of love and purpose, we first need to learn how to enter God's presence with the right spirit, approach, and preparation so that we can have this communion with Him.

"Entering into God's presence" is a term frequently used in the church today in reference to worship and prayer. However, in our casual, twenty-first-century Christianity, most of us don't understand what this concept really means. We often fall short of entering into God's presence because we lack a genuine reverence for Him. We need to be spiritually sensitive to the fact that God is holy, mighty, and worthy to be reverenced.

One of the favorite theological ideas in many churches today is that grace cancels law. Yet because we misunderstand the nature of grace, we are casual about our obedience to God. We commit sin, and then we hurriedly ask for forgiveness on our way to church or a prayer meeting. By the time we get to the gathering, we think we're ready to join with other believers in prayer. We treat the precious blood of Jesus, which He gave His life to deliver to us, as if it's some temporary covering for our messes so we can sin all over again. Sadly, we don't really love Jesus—we use Him. Then we wonder why God doesn't answer our prayers. The truth is that grace supersedes law in the sense that only the grace we receive in Christ enables us to *fulfill* God's law.

Jesus told us that the greatest commandment of all is, *"Love the Lord your God with all your heart and with all your soul and with all your mind"* (Matthew 22:37). God is saying to the church, in essence, "Don't obey Me because of the things you want from Me. Obey Me because you love Me. *'If you love me, you will obey what I command'* (John 14:15). If you love Me, you won't need chastisement and discipline to do what I ask of you."

God doesn't want us to use Him merely as safety insurance from hell. He wants a relationship, not a religion. He wants to be a Father to us. He wants communion with us. Communion means intimacy with our heavenly Father through which we receive His love, express our love for Him, find out His will, and then do it. It is entering into the very mind and heart of God in order to become one with Him and His purposes. Jesus prayed for us, *"That all of them may be one, Father, just as you are in me and I am in you. May they also be in us so that the world may believe that you have sent me"* (John 17:21).

⌒

Thought: We need to be spiritually sensitive to the fact that God is holy, mighty, and worthy to be reverenced.

Reading: 1 John 4:7–12

GOD IS HOLY

"Exalt the LORD our God and worship at his holy mountain, for the LORD our God is holy." —Psalm 99:9

As we continue to discuss how to enter into God's presence, we must talk further about His holiness. There is perhaps no word that describes God better than *holy.*

Holiness is critical to prayer because *"without holiness no one will see the Lord"* (Hebrews 12:14). Jesus emphasized this truth when He said, *"Blessed are the pure in heart, for they will see God"* (Matthew 5:8). I don't believe these verses refer to being in heaven after we die but to living everyday life on earth. They refer to seeing God now in the sense of having an intimate relationship of love with Him and entering into His presence so we can know His heart and mind. When Jesus said that the pure in heart will see God, He was teaching us the heart attitude by which we are to live every day—on this earth. He was telling us how to remain in unity with our Father.

What does it mean to be pure in heart? *Pure* means holy. Therefore, Jesus was saying, in effect, "Blessed are the holy in heart, for they will see God." The word *holy* means "sanctified, or set apart," or "set." "Blessed are the set in heart, for they will see God." When you are pure in heart, your mind is set on God and His ways.

"I am the LORD your God; consecrate yourselves [set yourselves apart] *and be holy, because I am holy"* (Leviticus 11:44). God is saying to you, "Set yourself in the same way that I set Myself; be holy, just as I am holy." To consecrate yourself means to position or

set yourself in such a way that you say, "I'm not going to stop until I get what I'm going after."

In addition, holiness always has to do with separation from whatever would draw us away from the Lord. *"You are to be holy to me because I, the LORD, am holy, and I have set you apart from the nations to be my own"* (Leviticus 20:26). Holiness has to do with fixing yourself—your heart and your mind—on God and not being influenced by people who are not set on Him and do not believe His Word.

How do holiness and seeing God relate to prayer? The Scriptures say, *"Stand still, and see the salvation of the LORD"* (Exodus 14:13 NKJV; see also 2 Chronicles 20:17 NKJV). God says, in essence, "If you are holy, then I will manifest Myself to you. You will see Me; you will see My salvation in your life." If your mind is set in regard to your prayer—that is, if you are convinced that God will do what He has promised you, if you are pure both in what you believe and in what you do—then you will see God manifested. In this sense, *holiness is the key* both to being persistent in prayer and to receiving answers to prayer. Holiness is being convinced that what God says and what God does are the same.

⌒

Thought: Holiness has to do with fixing yourself—your heart and your mind—on God and not being influenced by people who are not set on Him and do not believe His Word.

Reading: Leviticus 20:8

BE SINGLE-MINDED

"You will seek me and find me when you seek me with all your heart."   —Jeremiah 29:13

What does holiness mean to you? To some people, holiness means some mystical, nebulous, weird, smoky, cloudy presence. But holiness is very practical and real. Holiness means "one"— not the number one, but one in the sense of "complete." Holiness denotes the concept of being integrated. *Integrated* comes from the same word as *integrity*. God has integrity because who He is, what He says, what He does are the same. That's exactly what holiness means.

When we go to God in prayer, we must have the same integrity between what we say and do that He does, because holiness means telling the truth and then living the truth. God says, *"You will seek me and find me when you seek me with all your heart"* (Jeremiah 29:13). We can't just say we are seeking God; we must really be seeking Him, if we want to find Him. In other words, we must be single-minded in our desire to find Him. We must say, like Jacob, "God, I'm not going to let You go until I see you." (See Genesis 32:24–30.)

Is that the way you approach God? If you are single-minded and seek God with all your heart, mind, and conscience, if you seek Him with everything that is in you, He promises that you will find Him. It is because we know God is holy that we can believe He will fulfill what He has promised. We can believe we will receive what we ask of Him according to His Word.

If you are integrated, then what you say, what you believe, what you do, and how you respond are the same. However, if you tell God you believe Him but then act in the opposite way when you are on your job, taking care of your children, or with your friends, you are not integrated, pure, holy. You are double-minded. This is a crucial point for prayer: double-mindedness is the opposite of holiness and integrity. The apostle James warned us, *"When you ask, you must believe and not doubt, because the one who doubts is like a wave of the sea, blown and tossed by the wind. That person should not expect to receive anything from the Lord. Such a person is double-minded and unstable in all they do"* (James 1:6–8 NIV2011).

If we doubt God and His Word, we are being double-minded. That means that we don't have integrity—we're not integrated, not holy. Again, since God is holy, we must seek after holiness if we want to receive answers to our prayers.

Be single-minded—seek the Lord with all of your heart. He has promised that you will find Him. *"Come near to God and he will come near to you.... Purify your hearts, you double-minded"* (James 4:8).

⌣⌐

Thought: When we go to God in prayer, we must have the same integrity between what we say and do that He does, because holiness means telling the truth and then living the truth.

Reading: Genesis 32:24–30

A KINGDOM OF PRIESTS

"You will be for me a kingdom of priests and a holy nation."
—Exodus 19:6

Shortly after God delivered the Israelites from slavery in Egypt, He instructed Moses, "Go and tell the people, 'You will be for me *a kingdom of priests and a holy nation'"* (Exodus 19:6). Who were going to be priests? The entire nation of people, both male and female—children, teenagers, young adults, middle-aged adults, and the elderly—were all to be priests.

In God's perspective, the priesthood is ultimately not for a special group of people but for all those who belong to Him. This promise corresponds to His original plan for mankind to exercise dominion authority on the earth. Therefore, when God called the children of Israel *"a kingdom of priests and a holy nation,"* He was reflecting His purposes for mankind from Adam to Abraham to Jacob to the children of Israel and beyond. God's plan is that mankind be His priestly representative on earth.

However, we learn from Scripture that human beings failed as God's priests. Therefore, God raised up a Priest not only from the line of Abraham but also from His own house, One who would be faithful—Jesus, the second person of the Trinity, the Son of God, our High Priest:

> *No one takes this honor [of being a priest] upon himself; he must be called by God, just as Aaron was. So Christ also did not take upon himself the glory of becoming a high priest. But God said to him, "You are my Son; today I have become your Father." And he says in another place, "You are a priest forever, in the order of Melchizedek."* (Hebrews 5:4–6)

This Priest didn't fail. He served God perfectly. He knew how to enter God's presence and how to represent man to God and God to man. In doing so, He created a new nation of people who would be God's priests to the world. This nation is called the church. What did God say to the church? The same thing He had said to Israel. The apostle Peter wrote:

> You also, like living stones, are being built into a spiritual house
> to be a holy priesthood, offering spiritual sacrifices acceptable
> to God through Jesus Christ. (1 Peter 2:5)

Aaron, the first high priest, was a type of Christ—who became our High Priest in salvation. Even though Aaron's priesthood ultimately failed, he was still a model of the spiritual nation of priests who would serve God in Christ. There is much we can learn from God's instructions to Aaron that will help us understand our New Testament role as *"a royal priesthood"* (1 Peter 2:9). In the next devotion, we will discover ten steps God wants us to take to prepare to enter His presence.

⌒

Thought: God wants to win the world through a priesthood of believers.

Reading: 1 Peter 2:9–10

TEN STEPS TO PREPAREDNESS IN PRAYER

*"But you are a chosen people, a royal priesthood, a holy nation,
a people belonging to God, that you may declare the praises of
him who called you out of darkness into his wonderful light."*
—1 Peter 2:9

In Leviticus 16, God gave Aaron instructions for entering into His presence on the Day of Atonement. This passage reveals how God wants us to come into His presence today. Here are ten steps of preparedness to enable us to commune with God, offer effectual prayer, and be His mediators on behalf of the world:[5]

1. *Appropriate God's grace.* Acknowledge God's holiness, turn away from your sins, and be cleansed through the blood of Christ. (See Leviticus 16:3; 1 John 1:7–9.)

2. *Put on righteousness.* Appropriate the righteousness of Christ through faith. Live in that righteousness, doing what is right by keeping in step with the Spirit. (See Leviticus 16:4; Ephesians 4:24; 6:14; Galatians 5:25.)

3. *Put on truth and honesty.* Be transparent and clean before the Lord, desiring truth in the innermost parts and living with integrity. (See Leviticus 16:4; Psalm 51:6; Ephesians 6:14.)

4. *Cleanse yourself with the Word.* Before you come before God, make sure that you've *read* the Word, that the Word is *in* you, and that you are *obeying* the Word. (See Leviticus 16:4; Psalm 119:9–11.)

5. *Worship and praise God.* Honor and worship God in spirit and in truth, acknowledging Him as your all in all. (See Leviticus 16:12–13; John 4:19–24.)

---

5. For more detailed teaching on these ten steps of preparedness, please see *Understanding the Purpose and Power of Prayer*, 84–96.

6. *Separate yourself.* Remove yourself from your normal environment, activities, and distractions. Find the place in God where He meets you by coming to Him with the right heart, attitude, and motives. (See Leviticus 16:17; Jeremiah 29:13; Matthew 6:5–6.)

7. *Believe.* Have faith in God's power to do what He has promised and in the effectiveness of Christ's sacrifice. (See Leviticus 16:18–19; Hebrews 9:11–14.)

8. *Give God the glory.* Confess that God is the One who accomplished your atonement, forgiveness, and reconciliation with Him and is worthy to be praised. Give to others out of the abundance God has given you. (See Leviticus 16:25; Isaiah 42:8; 48:11.)

9. *Wash in the Word.* Ask God to fulfill His purposes based on His will and the promises in His Word. (See Leviticus 16:26; 2 Corinthians 1:20.)

10. *Remain in the anointing.* Remain in a state of preparedness for prayer. Honor the Lord by reflecting His nature and character in your life. (See Leviticus 16:32–34; 1 John 2:27.)

God is a God of holiness, and we aren't to approach Him in an offhand or careless way. It is important that we learn what it means to honor the Lord. Always remember that Jesus Christ has made it possible for us to fulfill each of these steps of preparation for prayer.

Heavenly Father,

Thank You for the privilege of being able to enter with confidence into the place where You dwell, because of the atonement that Your Son has made on our behalf. In Jesus's name, amen.

⌒

Thought: We must follow God's ways if we want to remain in His presence.

Reading: Leviticus 16

WHAT KIND OF FAITH ARE
YOU LIVING BY?

*"Clearly no one is justified before God by the law, because,
'The righteous will live by faith.'"* —Galatians 3:11

Previously, we talked about how many of us struggle with unanswered prayer. One reason why our prayers may fail to produce results is that we have the wrong kind of faith. I didn't say that we *lack* faith. I said we have the *wrong kind* of faith. Understanding the different kinds of faith, and how faith functions, are key preparations for prayer.

Every day, you and I live by faith. In fact, everyone lives by faith. But there is positive faith and there is negative faith. Both come by the same means—by what we listen to and what we believe.

Some type of faith is working in our lives, whether we are aware of it or not. If we are going to do any kind of business with God, we need to be able to function in the faith the Bible speaks of. *"Without faith it is impossible to please God"* (Hebrews 11:6). Many of us were taught that faith is necessary. However, we usually weren't taught how to obtain the faith that is pleasing to God.

First, let's define faith in general terms. The New Testament word *"faith"* comes from the Greek word *pistis*, which simply means "belief" or "confidence." Having faith means believing and having confidence in the words that you hear. It is believing in something that is not seen as though it is already a reality—and then speaking it and expecting it until it manifests itself. Everyone lives by this definition of faith, and people usually receive exactly what they have faith for. Why? Men and women were created in God's image to operate in the same way He does—through words of faith. *"For [God] spoke, and it came to be; he commanded, and it stood firm"* (Psalm 33:9).

God created everything by believing in the reality of what He would create before He saw its manifestation. *"By faith we understand that the universe was formed at God's command, so that what is seen was not made out of what was visible"* (Hebrews 11:3). God not only spoke words to create things, but He also uses words to keep the universe running. Hebrews 1:3 says, *"The Son is the radiance of God's glory and the exact representation of his being, sustaining all things by his powerful word."* God sustains everything by the power of His word. He spoke, and the universe came into being. He keeps on speaking, and this keeps the universe going.

The principle is this: When you ask for something in prayer, *you have to start speaking about it as if it already exists.* Moreover, you have to *keep on* speaking in order to see its manifestation. Then, when it comes, it is not enough to receive it from God. You have to be able to retain what God has blessed you with. How do you retain it? By speaking it. When the devil tries to steal it, you are to say, "No! Faith brought this to me; faith keeps it mine; this belongs to me!"

⌒

Thought: Men and women were created in God's image to operate in the same way He does—through words of faith.

Reading: Hebrews 11:3–6

THE WORD OF FAITH IS NEAR YOU

"But the righteousness of faith speaks in this way,…'The word is near you, in your mouth and in your heart' (that is, the word of faith which we preach)."　　—Romans 10:6, 8 (NKJV)

Romans 10:8 speaks of *"the word of faith."* Where is that word? It *"is near you, in your mouth and in your heart."*

I think the word *"near"* has to do with what you are listening to. When you turn on the television or tune into other media, words of faith—that is, words that create the raw material for your belief—are near you. The same process occurs when people talk to you. This means that the person sitting next to you is very influential. What they say to you goes into your ears. Your ears are the gateway to your heart, and *"out of the overflow of the heart the mouth speaks"* (Matthew 12:34).

What you say is a reflection of what is in your heart, of what you believe. As we discussed in the previous devotion, you will likely have what you say because God has given you the same ability He possesses—creative expression through your words. Just as God created His world with His words, so you create your world with your words. Again, every word reflects some type of faith. Thus, *faith is belief in action.*

In fact, faith is the greatest element in advanced civilization. What do I mean by this? Human faith has given birth to great achievement, and still does. Nothing in the world is more powerful than belief. All the people in the world who have ever dealt with human development agree with this truth. Why? Because belief creates your life, and that's what faith is: believing things that you haven't yet seen to the point that you act on them until they come into being. It is through faith that people experience personal growth and success.

This is a crucial truth for us to remember. Faith is active belief. It is belief combined with expectation and action. Once more, this is true of both positive and negative faith. Have you ever expected to fail and then failed? That's faith. You expect you are not going to get a loan, and so you talk yourself out of it on the way to the bank. You tell yourself all the reasons why you can't get it; you preach this to yourself, so that you say, "There's no use in my going, but let me try it anyway." When you don't get it, you confirm your belief by saying, "Just as I expected."

But prayer is the expression of man's dependency upon God for all things. God wants us to talk to Him. He wants us to pray in a way that reflects the faith He gives us through His Word—righteous faith—because such prayer is based on His good purposes for us.

⌒

Thought: Faith is active belief. It is belief combined with expectation and action.

Reading: Hebrews 11:1–2

—Day 28—

HAVE THE GOD KIND OF FAITH

"And without faith it is impossible to please God, because anyone who comes to him must believe that he exists and that he rewards those who earnestly seek him." —Hebrews 11:6

One of the most important illustrations in the Bible concerning faith and prayer is found in the book of Mark:

The next day as they were leaving Bethany, Jesus was hungry. Seeing in the distance a fig tree in leaf, he went to find out if it had any fruit. When he reached it, he found nothing but leaves, because it was not the season for figs. Then he said to the tree, "May no one ever eat fruit from you again." And his disciples heard him say it. (Mark 11:12–14)

What did Jesus do in this situation? He used words. What kind of words did He use? Words of faith. Remember that faith is active belief. When He spoke to the tree, Jesus actively believed that the tree would die.

What happened to the tree Jesus spoke to? *"In the morning, as they went along, they saw the fig tree withered from the roots. Peter remembered and said to Jesus, 'Rabbi, look! The fig tree you cursed has withered!'"* (Mark 11:20–21). Most translations give Jesus's reply as, *"Have faith in God"* (verse 22). Yet that is not the way it was written in the original Greek. The literal translation is, "Have the God kind of faith."

What you hear creates faith for what you are hearing. Then you speak it, and it happens to you. That is why Jesus said that if we want to operate as He does, we must have the "God kind of faith":

I tell you the truth, if anyone says to this mountain, "Go, throw yourself into the sea" and does not doubt in his heart but believes that what he says will happen, it will be done for him. Therefore I tell you, whatever you ask for in prayer, believe that you have received it, and it will be yours.

(Mark 11:23–24)

The Bible says, *"Faith comes by hearing"* (Romans 10:17 NKJV). Faith doesn't just initially come by hearing. It *continues to come* by continual hearing. I can't stress this truth enough. If you listen to good teaching for one hour and then listen to negative talk for two hours, you are going to have faith for the negative. Remember, faith comes from the word that is near you. (See Romans 10:8.) That is why I'm careful about the company I keep. I want to be around people who speak words that produce the *faith of God* because this is the kind of faith we are to have.

We need to be aware continually that there are other kinds of faith all around us besides the God kind of faith. I encourage you to check the company you're keeping; check what you're listening to, and who you're listening to; check the books you read, the music you listen to, the movies and videos you watch, and the church you attend—because you will become what you listen to and will speak what you hear!

⌒

Thought: Faith doesn't just initially come by hearing. It *continues to come* by continual hearing.

Reading: Luke 18:1–8

GOD'S FAITH COMES BY HIS WORD

"The word of faith we are proclaiming: that if you confess with your mouth, 'Jesus is Lord,' and believe in your heart that God raised him from the dead, you will be saved."
—Romans 10:8–9

Consider these questions: "What do you say when you're in the midst of trouble?" "What do you say when there is adversity?" "What do you say when things are not going the way you want them to go?"

During such times, what you have been listening to will come out of your mouth because that is what is in your heart. This is why it's so important to have a constant diet of the Word of God; you have to let it get down into your heart. It will nourish your heart so that, when you experience troubles, the Word is what will come out of your mouth, and you will create what the Word says.

Romans 10:8 tells us, *"The word is near you; it is in your mouth and in your heart."* In this instance, we could define *"heart"* as the subconscious mind. It's where you store everything you have been listening to. Again, what comes out of your mouth creates your world because you are just like God in the way you function. Whatever you speak has the power to happen.

How is a person saved? By confessing with the mouth and believing in the heart. Paul said the word that is near you is *"the word of faith we are proclaiming: that if you confess with your mouth, 'Jesus is Lord,' and believe in your heart that God raised him from the dead, you will be saved"* (Romans 10:8–9). Being born again is difficult for some people to understand because they think there has to be a feeling connected with the supernatural activity of God. In other words, they say, "I prayed this prayer for salvation, but I don't feel anything." That is where they are in error. The Bible says that if a person wants to be saved, he needs to believe and speak—not feel.

You must understand this truth because it is crucial to your life and your prayers. Your salvation came by the confession of your mouth and the belief in your heart. When you confessed your faith in the Lord Jesus, He actually, in reality, without a doubt, *became your Lord*. In light of this truth, consider the following: if you are born again by your words, if you can be kept out of hell and can go to heaven by your words, if there is that much power in what you say, then what effect are the rest of the words you speak having on you? Please remember this: you can be *positively* or *negatively* affected by what you say and believe. (See Proverbs 18:21.)

How does this principle apply to prayer? What you keep saying the most is what you will receive. If you pray for something, and then you start saying the opposite, you will get what you say. If you pray according to the Word of God, and keep standing on the Word, you will have what you ask for and what God wills for your life.

‿⁀

Thought: A constant diet of the Word of God will nourish your heart.

Reading: Psalm 119:105

— DAY 30 —

JESUS IS LORD!

"If you confess with your mouth, 'Jesus is Lord,' and believe in your heart that God raised him from the dead, you will be saved." —Romans 10:9

Today, we return to the declaration *"Jesus is Lord"* from Romans 10:9. Since knowing Jesus as Lord is vital for our salvation and has significant implications for prayer, we want to consider this proclamation carefully.

The word *lord* means "proprietor" or "owner." If we substitute the word *owner* for *"Lord"* in the above passage, we can say that we are saved by confessing with our mouths, "Jesus is my Owner! He owns all of my life: lock, stock, and barrel; body, mind, and spirit; past, present, and future. He owns my body; I can't take my body just anywhere I want to any longer. He owns my mind; I can't put just anything I want to into my mind anymore. He owns my spirit; there's no room for the devil there. He owns my car; I can't use it to do anything negative or evil. He owns my house; I can't do anything immoral in it." In other words, if Jesus is truly your Lord, then it will show up in your attitudes and actions.

We read in 1 Corinthians, *"You know that when you were pagans, somehow or other you were influenced and led astray to mute idols. Therefore I tell you that no one who is speaking by the Spirit of God says, 'Jesus be cursed,' and no one can say, 'Jesus is Lord,' except by the Holy Spirit"* (1 Corinthians 12:2–3). You are saved by confessing, *"Jesus is Lord,"* and you cannot say this unless the Holy Spirit enables you to. You cannot fake this confession—saying that Jesus is your Lord and then doing only what you feel like doing. If you say that Jesus is your Lord, but you aren't living as if He owns your life, you are insulting Him.

You probably know people who say they are believers, who claim they have accepted Christ as Lord, but whose lifestyle hasn't changed. They are still coveting, gossiping, lying, stealing, drinking, using drugs, or living in adultery, but then they go to church and take communion. They say that Jesus is their Lord, but they are not living by the Spirit of Christ.

When you truly confess and believe, "Jesus is my Lord," all heaven goes into action to make sure you receive the Holy Spirit because heaven recognizes the word of faith. Then, after you make your confession, it needs to remain a reality in your life. You need to continue affirming, "Jesus is my Lord." God knows if you are serious about your confession because only the Holy Spirit can confirm it.

"For it is with your heart that you believe and are justified, and it is with your mouth that you confess and are saved. As the Scripture says, 'Anyone who trusts in him will never be put to shame'" (Romans 10:10–11). When you say that Jesus is your Lord, you have to trust that He truly is. If you keep believing that and saying that, the Bible says you will not be made ashamed.

In the next devotion, we will talk further about how the same principle applies to prayer.

⌣

Thought: If Jesus is truly your Lord, then it will show up in your attitudes and actions.

Reading: Philippians 2:5–11

PLANTED BY THE WORD

"The righteous will flourish like a palm tree...; planted in the house of the LORD, they will flourish in the courts of our God." —Psalm 92:12–13

I want to further connect the principle of the word of faith with our approach to prayer. If you ask God to make a way for you concerning a situation on your job or a relationship or an idea He's given you for a business—if you believe it, confess it, and hold on to God's truth concerning your situation—you will not be made ashamed.

God has promised that if we live righteously and delight in His Word, we will be *"like a tree planted by streams of water, which yields its fruit in season and whose leaf does not wither,"* and that whatever we do will prosper. (See Psalm 1:3.) You can claim that Scripture for yourself. If you say these words in prayer, and then you keep saying them and believing them, God promises, "You won't be made ashamed concerning them."

In the Bible, water is used as a symbol of the Word of God. The tree mentioned in Psalm 1:3 is *"planted by streams of water."* It is healthy and yields fruit because it is near the water and can draw the water by its roots. In the same way, you have to be connected to the Word of God so it can flow continuously into your life. Then you will bear *your* fruit in its season. You might not see the answer to your prayer at the moment, but the season is coming because the Word is flowing into your life. Anyone who has been questioning your trust in God is going to see your fruit. Your season is on the way. You can say, "I haven't seen any results yet, but there's fruit in the tree!"

How do you keep believing? You have to be planted. Plant yourself in a place where the Word is prevalent and the people around you are continually speaking and living it. The more time you spend in the Word, the more your mind is transformed. You begin thinking differently. When you are constantly around something, when you keep hearing it, it becomes a part of your heart. You start believing it, and that belief is reflected in what you say. Then the fruit starts coming.

Some of the things you are praying for right now have not been manifested because it is not yet their season. Therefore, between the seed prayer and the manifestation of the fruit, you have to stay on the riverbank, reading, meditating on, speaking, living, breathing the Word. Plant yourself!

When you trust in God and believe what He has promised you, God says that He's going to vindicate you in the end. He's going to make you such a blessing that people are going to shake their heads and say, "Tell me about your God." Then you can pass along the power of the word of faith to others!

Thought: You have to be connected to the Word of God so it can flow continuously into your life.

Reading: Psalm 1

— Day 32 —

FAITH IS YOUR TITLE DEED

*"Faith is being sure of what we hope for and certain of what we
do not see."* —Hebrews 11:1

Faith is your title deed to what God has promised. A title deed is
the evidence or proof of a person's legal ownership. Therefore, faith
is the proof of your ownership of what you are praying for.

However, you must make sure you are exercising the God kind
of faith. Jesus said, *"If you remain in me and my words remain in you,
ask whatever you wish, and it will be given you"* (John 15:7). In effect,
He was saying, "Tell Me what I tell you." The God kind of faith
puts its full trust in God's Word.

In Matthew 16, when Jesus explained to His disciples that
He would need to suffer and die but would be raised again on the
third day, Peter began to rebuke Him, saying that would never
happen to Him. (See verses 21–22.) What was Jesus's response?
He immediately reproved Peter, saying, *"Get behind me, Satan! You
are a stumbling block to me; you do not have in mind the things of God,
but the things of men"* (Matthew 16:23).

Jesus was hearing Peter say something that contradicted
God's will. Therefore, He told Peter, in essence, "Your words are
contrary to Mine. You are being a temptation to Me!" Peter was
speaking something that was not of God. He was speaking the
wrong language. It is interesting to note that Peter later referred to
Satan as the *"adversary"* (1 Peter 5:8 KJV, NKJV). The Greek word
for *"adversary"* means "opponent." Satan is the one who speaks
the opposite of God's Word. We must be careful not to speak the
wrong language by praying for something adverse to God's Word.
We also need to be careful not to listen to people who tell us what

is contrary to the Word or why something can't be done, when God has said it can. Satan's goal is to feed you words contrary to God's words, thereby producing faith for destruction and death.

Keep believing and talking about the goodness of God and the impossibilities that God can bring to pass. The Bible says God fulfills His Word and *"calls things that are not as though they were"* (Romans 4:17). Affirm in your heart, "This is the beginning of a new lifestyle of faith for me—the God kind of faith." All prayer must be the prayer of faith!

Let's pray together:

Heavenly Father,

The Bible says, *"'The word is near you; it is in your mouth and in your heart,' that is, the word of faith"* (Romans 10:8). We pray that we will place our trust in You and Your Word rather than in the words of faith all around us that are contrary to Your truth. Forgive us for spending more time dwelling on our own plans, ideas, scenarios, analyses, and schemes than taking Your Word into our hearts and living by it. Open the truths of Your Word to us and let us rely on You alone. We pray this in the name of Jesus, who is the Living Word. Amen.

Thought: The Word of God needs to be the source we listen to for our faith.

Reading: 1 Peter 1:8–9

A LIFESTYLE OF PRAYER

"Now it came to pass in those days that He went out to the mountain to pray, and continued all night in prayer to God."
—Luke 6:12 (NKJV)

The secret to Jesus's success in ministry was a lifestyle of prayer.

Of all the things Jesus's disciples observed Him say and do, the Bible records only one thing they asked Him to teach them, and that was how to pray. (See Luke 11:1.) I believe that was because they saw Jesus pray more than anything else. The disciples lived with Jesus. They went everywhere He went and observed Him for three and a half years. Based on the Scriptures, we can deduce that Christ prayed for approximately four to five hours every morning. He also prayed at other times.

The Scripture says, *"Very early in the morning, while it was still dark ["rising up a great while before day" KJV], Jesus got up, left the house and went off to a solitary place, where he prayed"* (Mark 1:35). While the disciples were sleeping, Jesus was praying. Then the disciples would get up and say, "Where's the Master?" When they eventually found Him, He would be praying. They saw this every morning. He would spend five hours with God His Father. Then He would say, "Let's go to Jerusalem," or somewhere else, where He would spend minutes or even seconds healing people or casting out demons.

Notice the ratio: He spent five hours doing one thing and a few minutes or seconds doing the other. He continually operated in that manner. The church today hasn't yet understood this truth. We spend a few minutes with God, and then we try to do many hours of work in His name.

Martin Luther started the Reformation that created the Protestant movement and changed the course of the world. He said something to the effect of, "When I have a lot to do in a day, I spend more time in prayer, because more work is done by prayer than by work itself." He was right. If I am too busy to pray, I am too busy. If you are too busy to pray, you are too busy.

We can never really be too busy to pray because prayer makes our lives much more focused, efficient, and peaceful. Learning this principle has been essential in my life. When I have many things on my heart and mind, a lot of confusion in my life, or overwhelming circumstances to face, I don't try to tackle these problems myself. I go to God in prayer, and He gives me the wisdom and guidance I need to address them.

Jesus was succinct in His knowledge of what was important because He spent time with the Father in prayer. We do many things in our days that God didn't plan for us to do. One hour with Him could accomplish ten hours of work because we wouldn't be dealing with trial and error any longer. God would tell us what is really important, compared to what seems urgent. God would supernaturally give us wisdom to address our situations.

Prayer will give you discernment that you wouldn't otherwise have. It will enable you to think clearly and wisely.

Thought: Hours with God make minutes with men effective.

Reading: Luke 6:12–19

— DAY 34 —

INTIMACY WITH THE FATHER

"My Father has been working until now, and I have been working." —John 5:17 (NKJV)

In John 5:1–9, we read that Jesus did a great miracle beside a pool in Bethesda. He healed a man who had been sick for thirty-eight years—and He did it on the Sabbath. How did people react to this healing? Some were deeply impressed. Some were angry. Others wanted answers. Jesus explained something to them that many of us are still trying to grasp. When I discovered the deep truth that Jesus was teaching here, it changed my whole life—including my perspective of myself and my relationship to the Father.

The account continues, *"So, because Jesus was doing these things on the Sabbath, the Jews persecuted him. Jesus said to them, 'My Father is always at his work to this very day, and I, too, am working'"* (verses 16–17). The *New King James Version* reads, *"My Father has been working until now, and I have been working."*

In effect, Christ was saying to those who questioned His healing, "I spent time with My Father this morning. I already had my whole day worked out for Me because I had fellowship with the One who made days. My Father has already healed the people I'm touching. Their healing is the result of My knowing what My Father is doing. I'm just manifesting it. My Father works; therefore, I work." In essence, what we do should be a manifestation of what God the Father has already done.

What a way to live! "This morning, in prayer, I saw this sick man healed; so, this afternoon, I have come to heal him." Why? "My Father has already cleansed him. I have come to manifest it."

Look at the next verse in this account: *"For this reason the Jews tried all the harder to kill him; not only was he breaking the Sabbath, but he was even calling God his own Father, making himself equal with God"* (John 5:18). In other words, Jesus was saying that God was His personal, intimate Source. His detractors couldn't take that.

Jesus explained to them how His intimacy with the Father worked. *"I tell you the truth, the Son can do nothing by himself; he can do only what he sees his Father doing, because whatever the Father does the Son also does. For the Father loves the Son and shows him all he does"* (verses 19–20). Again, we spend most of our time during the day trying to figure out what God wants us to do, and we waste the whole day. Christ is saying to us, "I go to the Father first; I see what He's already done, and I do it." This is the pattern He wants us to follow.

Many Christians think the length of time we pray isn't important. Then why did Jesus spend hours in prayer? It is because He had a genuine relationship with His Father, and any relationship takes time to build and maintain. Will you spend time with the Father in prayer to develop a deeper relationship with Him?

⌣

Thought: We often discover that when we spend time in prayer, God begins to use *us* to change the circumstances around us.

Reading: John 5:1–14

—Day 35—

MANIFESTING GOD'S THOUGHTS

"For I have come down from heaven not to do my will but to do the will of him who sent me."   —John 6:38

Prayer is coming into union with God's mind. God showed Jesus everything He was thinking and said to His Son, "Go and manifest that for Me."

There is nothing more intimate than our thoughts. Words are an extension of our thoughts, but we *are* our thoughts. Proverbs 23:7 says, *"As [a person] thinks in his heart, so is he"* (NKJV). God desires not to talk to you but to "think" to you. This is what Jesus meant when He essentially said, "I do what I see My Father doing." (See John 5:19.) The text implies, "I do what I mentally see My Father thinking."

A thought is a silent word. A word is a manifested thought. Jesus was saying, "When I go before God in prayer and spend time with Him, He gives Me His thoughts." Therefore, when Jesus was asked why He healed the sick man at the pool (see John 5:1–9), He said, in effect, "I just saw that thought this morning. I am the Word. I manifest the thoughts of God. I have to heal this man because that is what I saw."

Every time Jesus talked about His work, He kept mentioning the love of His Father. In essence, Jesus was indicating, "My Father loves Me so much that He does not just talk to Me; He *communes* with Me. He loves Me so much that He speaks to My spirit and mind. The reason I spend time with Him in the morning is to find out what He is thinking, what is on His mind."

Ninety-nine percent of the time, God will speak to your mind through your spirit. Many people are waiting for a burning-bush experience or the appearance of an angel. They don't hear from God because they're waiting in the wrong way. God doesn't generally speak verbally. That's not intimate enough. He speaks directly to our spirits.

Jesus was naturally supernatural. He would walk up to a man and say, "How long have you been sick?" "Thirty-eight years." "Fine. Take up your bed and walk." Everybody would be fascinated watching this Man work. He would walk down the street, meet a woman who was bent over, and say, "Straighten up," and she would straighten up. He would walk a little further and say to someone, "Are you blind?" "Yes." He would touch the person's eyes, and the person would see. The religious people said, "Wait a minute. You're supposed to say, 'Stand back, everybody. I'm getting ready to perform a miracle.'" Religious people spend a long time preparing when they attempt to do miracles. Christ just walked around, spoke, touched—and things happened. People became angry with Jesus because they thought He wasn't spiritual enough. He was spiritual long before they knew. Remember, He was spiritual for five hours so He could be natural for one minute.

⌣

Thought: Words are an extension of our thoughts, but we *are* our thoughts.

Reading: John 6:36–39

— Day 36 —

HEARING FROM GOD

"He who belongs to God hears what God says." —John 8:47

When you have an important decision to make—to take a certain job, start a business, go to a specific college, or get married—spend some time with God. He is going to make it easy for you. He helps you avoid making mistakes and doing things twice. Jesus wants us to operate in the way He operated: much time spent in communion and love with the Father, and much accomplished for the kingdom. Jesus specifically prayed that we would follow His example in this:

> *That all of them may be one, Father, just as you are in me and I am in you. May they also be in us so that the world may believe that you have sent me. I have given them the glory that you gave me, that they may be one as we are one.*
>
> (John 17:21–22)

The Father loves you, and He wants the same communion or "common-union" with you that He had with Jesus. Your prayer life can make you so intimate with God that you will walk around and naturally manifest the works, or thoughts, of God, just as Jesus did.

Jesus's detractors said, in effect, "Why did You call God Your Father? Why do You say He speaks to You? That's blasphemy. You cannot be that close to God." (See John 5:16–18.) Let me tell you that God has never appeared to me, but I hear from Him all the time. I have heard God's voice audibly only a few times in my entire life. The rest of His communication to me has been thoughts, ideas, impressions, suggestions in my heart, sensing, and discernment.

All of it was God speaking. Jesus's continual reference to "the Father" is critical, because the word *Father* is the Hebrew word *Abba,* which means "source and sustainer."

What are you looking for from God when you pray? Do you want a prophet to come from a far country to deliver a message from Him? When you love someone, you don't want to receive just a letter; you want to be close to them. You want to be intimate with that person. Jesus's relationship with the Father was so intimate that most people didn't understand how He spoke with such wisdom and did such miracles. I imagine the people were so impressed that they said to themselves, "He must be doing something we don't know about."

The disciples knew Jesus's secret because they observed His lifestyle of prayer. That is why they said, in effect, "Lord, don't teach us to do miracles; teach us to pray." If we learn what they learned, we're going to do the things Jesus did.

Thought: The Father loves you, and He wants the same communion or "common-union" with you that He had with Jesus.

Reading: Isaiah 30:21

PRAYER MUST BE LEARNED

"One day Jesus was praying in a certain place. When he finished, one of his disciples said to him, 'Lord, teach us to pray, just as John taught his disciples.'" —Luke 11:1

The above Scripture says, first of all, *"One day **Jesus** was praying."* The disciples were present, but they were not involved. Only Jesus was praying. What were they doing? They were observing Him.

Whenever the Bible mentions Jesus praying, it tells specific things about His actions. Let's look at some examples:

After he had dismissed them, he went up on a mountainside by himself to pray. When evening came, he was there alone.
(Matthew 14:23)

One of those days Jesus went out to a mountainside to pray, and spent the night praying to God. (Luke 6:12)

Very early in the morning, while it was still dark, Jesus got up, left the house and went off to a solitary place, where he prayed. (Mark 1:35)

Christ never seemed to pray with the disciples. I believe that was intentional on His part. He wanted them to ask Him about the most important aspect of His ministry. I also believe He prayed alone to teach us that prayer is a personal and private relationship and responsibility. Corporate prayer should never be a substitute for personal and private time with the Father.

Second, Luke 11:1 tells us that one of the disciples said, *"Lord, teach us to pray."* This request implies the disciples didn't think prayer was something they could do without Jesus's instruction. As young Jewish men, the disciples had been brought up in the synagogue and the temple, where they had been taught to pray. A part of their daily ritual was to pray in the synagogue, so they were always reading off prayers and repeating prayers. However, Jesus's prayers were different from what they were used to. They saw that there was something distinct about them. They prayed, but He *prayed.* They were busy, but He *obtained results.*

Third, this passage says that Jesus started to teach His disciples to pray. He began, *"When you pray...."* (Luke 11:2). This means Jesus agreed that the disciples needed to learn how to pray. He confirmed that prayer is not automatic but rather a function that must be taught. A new believer may say, "Well, I've never prayed in my life. I do not know how to pray." They are often told, "Just talk to God and tell Him how you feel." That sounds good—but that's not what Jesus taught His disciples.

Prayer is not just "talking to God." I used to teach that. I also used to do that, and nothing happened! I had to learn what Jesus instructed His disciples before I could become effective in prayer. There is a way we are to pray, and it has to be learned. In the next several devotions, we will explore what Jesus taught His disciples about prayer.

⌣

Thought: Prayer is a personal and private relationship and responsibility.

Reading: Matthew 6:5–15

A PATTERN FOR PRAYER

"[Jesus] said to them, 'When you pray, say: Our Father in heaven....'" —Luke 11:2 (NKJV)

I t is very important for us to realize that, regardless of the name it has been given, what Jesus taught His disciples about prayer is not really "the Lord's Prayer." It is a *model* for prayer. In other words, you don't need to repeat the words of this prayer exactly; instead, you should use them as a pattern.

As we've seen, prayer is approaching God in order to ask Him to accomplish His will on the earth. Christ taught His disciples how to fulfill this purpose. In doing so, He gave them this model to follow:

Our Father in heaven, hallowed be Your name. Your kingdom come. Your will be done on earth as it is in heaven. Give us day by day our daily bread. And forgive us our sins, for we also forgive everyone who is indebted to us. And do not lead us into temptation, but deliver us from the evil one.

(Luke 11:2–4 NKJV)

"Our Father." The first thing we learn is that we never bring only ourselves to prayer. When we approach God, we are to bring other people's concerns with us. Most of us go to prayer with our own shopping lists: our financial lists, our career lists, and many other things. We say, "Oh, Lord, please do these things for me." There is selfishness in such a prayer if we don't also pray for others. God will ask, "Where is everybody else? Where is your love and concern for the corporate needs of humanity? All men and women are My concern." Therefore, we are to begin prayer by thinking of

others as well as ourselves. The very first statement of the model excludes most of our prayers, doesn't it?

"*Our **Father**.*" Second, we address God as "Father." We identify who He is. As we saw earlier, one definition of the word *father* is "source." We are to go to God with the awareness and confession that He is the Source who can provide for the needs of everyone. Whatever your problem, the Father has the answer. He is *"Abba"* (Mark 14:36), the Source.

"*Our Father **in heaven**.*" Next, Jesus is saying, "When you pray, remember that you're not praying to someone on earth." Why is this important? Because earth is where the problem is. You need external help. God is in heaven. You are on earth in order to fulfill His plans for the world. In addition, if the Father is not on earth, we need an intermediary. We have to depend on Jesus and the Holy Spirit to be our intermediaries with God. (See, for example, Romans 8:26–27, 34.) Thus, when you say, *"Our Father in heaven,"* you're expressing to God, "I recognize that I need help from outside my realm." It is actually a confession of submission. "You're greater than all of us, O Lord. We need Your help."

⌒

Thought: We need help from outside our earthly realm—we need God's help—and we depend on Jesus and the Spirit as our intermediaries with God.

Reading: Psalm 121:1–2

— DAY 39 —

HALLOWED BE YOUR NAME

"Hallowed be Your name. Your kingdom come. Your will be done on earth as it is in heaven." —Luke 11:2 (NKJV)

Jesus's pattern for prayer continues, *"Hallowed be Your name."*

The word *hallowed* means reverenced, set apart, or sanctified. This indicates we are to begin our prayers by worshipping the Father as the Holy One. When you pray, you are to make God's name holy by honoring all the attributes of His holiness, such as His love, faithfulness, integrity, and grace. You worship. You adore. You exalt. You magnify. You deify. You glorify. After you pray, you continue to honor God in your life and in all your interactions with others.

How many times have you said, "I don't understand how people can pray for long periods of time. I run out of words to say; I run out of things to pray for"? If your answer is "Many times," that's because you haven't known how to pray. Prayer is not giving God a long list of requests. Jesus says, in essence, "Begin by acknowledging that the Father is your all in all, and worship Him." We will never run out of things for which to worship and praise God.

"Your kingdom come. Your will be done on earth as it is in heaven." This statement simply means that a true person of prayer is not interested in his own kingdom. His interest is in God's kingdom and what He wants accomplished. We should always ask for the fulfillment of God's prayer list before our own. What a reverse of how we usually do things!

We are to ask, "Father, what do You want done? What do You want to happen on earth?" God is delighted when you are excited about the things He's excited about. He will bless you in the course of accomplishing His work on earth. You don't have to worry about having your needs met if you start praying for God's will to be done on earth in other people's lives. God likes it when you bring other people's requests to Him and ask Him to meet their needs.

Again, that's why you are to pray, "**Our** Father." When you pray for other people, God will bless you because He will see that you have aligned your will with His will, that you are reaching out to others in love and compassion. He is going to answer your own requests because you are obeying Him. He will say, in effect, "I like this person. He isn't selfish. I'm going to make sure his own needs are met."

James 5:16 emphasizes this truth: "*Pray for each other so that you may be healed.*" This statement means that when you minister to someone else, God turns around and ministers to what you need. Isn't that just like God? "*Give, and it will be given to you*" (Luke 6:38). Therefore, if you are having problems, find someone else who has problems and start helping them solve theirs. If you need someone to pray for you, start praying for someone else. If you need financial help, give to someone who has less than you do. Jesus says to us, "Think about God's kingdom first."

Thought: When you pray for other people, God will bless you because He will see that you are reaching out to others in love and compassion.

Reading: Galatians 6:2

— DAY 40 —

GIVE US OUR DAILY BREAD

"Give us day by day our daily bread."   —Luke 11:3 (NKJV)

With the above statement from His model prayer, Jesus is saying, "While you are in God's presence and are asking Him to be faithful to fulfill His will on earth, include this request." We are to pray, *"Give us day by day our daily bread."* The plural pronoun used in this statement is tied to the *"Our"* in *"Our Father."* If you tell God that you are coming to Him with the concerns of other people, then, when you ask for bread, you have to ask for bread for everybody. We normally say, "Lord, provide for me." We're not thinking of anyone else. Yet God tells us once more, "Ask for others as well as yourself. Pray for others."

In Jesus's day, the term "daily bread" was a cultural idiom that referred to everything necessary for the making of bread. Therefore, when you say, *"Give us day by day our daily bread,"* you're praying not only for food but also for the whole process that is necessary to make the food possible. For example, to make bread, you need sunshine, rain, seed, nitrogen, oxygen, soil, nutrients, minerals, time, growth, harvesting, grinding, ingredients to add to the grain, mixing, kneading, and baking. Implied in those elements and steps are strength for the farmer to be able to sow and harvest the grain and strength for the one who mixes and kneads the bread. Jesus is talking about all that. In other words, you are praying for healthy bodies and a healthy environment in which food can grow.

"Give us day by day our daily bread" is a loaded statement. It teaches us to pray, "Thank You, Lord, for keeping the air in our country pollution-free. Thank You for making us wise people who

keep our beaches clean. Thank You for preserving the soil from oil contamination. Thank You for keeping all the nutrients in our soil rich, with no chemicals to harm them." We need to be praying in this way. We're not specific enough. We take too much for granted and don't ask God to protect and bless what we need for daily living—not only for our own sake, but also for the sake of others.

> *The eyes of all look to you, and you give them their food at the proper time. You open your hand and satisfy the desires of every living thing.* (Psalm 145:15–16)

Thought: We are to ask God to supply the daily needs of others as well as our own.

Reading: Matthew 6:25–33

— Day 41 —

FORGIVE US OUR SINS,
FOR WE ALSO FORGIVE

"And forgive us our sins, for we also forgive everyone who is indebted to us." —Luke 11:4 (NKJV)

Jesus is now dealing with forgiveness and relationships. He says, "Your prayer has to take into consideration those with whom you are in relationship." When you come before God, check to see if anyone has anything against you or if you are holding anything against anyone. Don't come into God's presence and expect to have your prayers answered if you are asking God to forgive you, but you are refusing to forgive others.

The gospel of Matthew includes this sobering statement after Jesus's teaching on prayer: *"For if you forgive men when they sin against you, your heavenly Father will also forgive you. But if you do not forgive men their sins, your Father will not forgive your sins"* (Matthew 6:14–15). And if God doesn't forgive you, He's not going to answer your prayer.

We often overlook the importance of our relationships—and how those relationships affect our prayers. However, as far as Christ is concerned, having good relationships is one of the keys to answered prayer:

Therefore, if you are offering your gift at the altar and there remember that your brother has something against you, leave your gift there in front of the altar. First go and be reconciled to your brother; then come and offer your gift.

(Matthew 5:23–24)

We can't do business at a holy altar when we have bitter hearts. We are to forgive freely. *"Peter came to Jesus and asked, 'Lord, how many times shall I forgive my brother when he sins against me? Up to seven times?' Jesus answered, 'I tell you, not seven times, but seventy-seven times'"* (Matthew 18:21–22).

When you pray and fast, God will reveal to you all the hurt, bitterness, and anger you are holding against people. There is going to be conviction in your life because God will remind you of broken relationships you had forgotten about. Why? Because He can talk to you about them now. He can finally get through to you because you're listening.

Perhaps you say, "I have faith to believe that God will answer my prayer," but you're holding on to unforgiveness. The Bible says, *"The only thing that counts is faith expressing itself through love"* (Galatians 5:6). So, God will say to you, "Yes, but faith works when love is in order, and you are not living in forgiveness."

Ask yourself these questions: "Have I committed a wrong against anybody?" "Am I holding on to a grudge?" "Is there anyone in my family, local church, or job with whom I am not in good relationship?" God is looking for clean hands and a pure heart. (See Psalm 24:3–4.) When we forgive others, God will also forgive us—and the way will be opened for Him to hear and answer our prayers.

⌒

Thought: We can't do business at a holy altar when we have a bitter heart.

Reading: Ephesians 4:32

— Day 42 —

DO NOT LEAD US INTO TEMPTATION

"And do not lead us into temptation, but deliver us from the evil one."   —Luke 11:4 (NKJV)

This last statement in Jesus's model prayer does not imply that God might steer us toward temptation against our wills. It means that we are to ask God for wisdom so we won't put ourselves into situations that will cause us to compromise our relationship with Him. In other words, we are to ask God for strength and wisdom to stop making bad decisions and to stop going into bad situations that will tempt us to sin. Some of us set ourselves up for trouble; then we ask God to deliver us. God is saying, "When you come before Me, pray for wisdom so you can make good decisions without compromising your life in any way."

When Jesus asked Peter, James, and John to stay with Him while He prayed in the garden of Gethsemane before His arrest and crucifixion, the disciples fell asleep. "*'Could you men not keep watch with me for one hour?' [Jesus] asked Peter. 'Watch and pray so that you will not fall into temptation. The spirit is willing, but the body is weak'*" (Matthew 26:40–41). Jesus knew that Peter was about to be tempted to deny Him—after claiming that he would be willing to die with Him. He told Peter to remain alert and pray. So, Jesus was referring to watchfulness and prayer when He taught us to say, "*Do not lead us into temptation.*"

We need to be alert to the temptations and weaknesses that could harm our relationship with God and our testimony for Him, things that Satan could exploit to cause us to stumble. Then we need to pray that God will protect us from succumbing to them. The Bible says, "*Put on the full armor of God so that you can take your stand against the devil's schemes*" (Ephesians 6:11).

Some of the biblical manuscripts include this benediction at the end of Jesus's teaching on prayer in Matthew's gospel: *"For Yours is the kingdom and the power and the glory forever. Amen"* (Matthew 6:13 NKJV). After you have prayed, then worship the Father again. When you do so, you're saying to God, "I know You're going to answer this prayer; therefore, I'm going to thank You ahead of time. I'm going to give You all the glory that comes from what happens. When the answer is manifested, I'm going to tell everybody that it is because of You." All the power and all the glory belong to God forever and ever!

⌒

Thought: We must be alert to temptations and weaknesses that Satan could exploit to harm our relationship with God.

Reading: 1 Peter 5:8–9

— DAY 43 —

DID THE DISCIPLES LEARN JESUS'S SECRET?

"After they prayed, the place where they were meeting was shaken. And they were all filled with the Holy Spirit and spoke the word of God boldly." —Acts 4:31

Jesus's disciples observed His lifestyle of prayer and asked Him to teach them to pray. Do we have any evidence that they learned His secret?

In Acts 1:14, we read that after Jesus was resurrected and had ascended to heaven, the disciples and the other followers of Jesus *"all continued with one accord in prayer and supplication"* (KJV, NKJV). They were waiting for the *"power from on high"* (Luke 24:49) that Jesus had promised them—and they were "watching and praying," just as He had taught them. (See Matthew 26:41.)

On the day of Pentecost, God filled the disciples with His Holy Spirit. At the outpouring of the Spirit, three thousand people were converted and *"everyone was filled with awe, and many wonders and miraculous signs were done by the apostles"* (Acts 2:43). The disciples' prayers resulted in their receiving the baptism of the Holy Spirit and working wonders and signs to God's glory, just as Jesus had done.

In the fourth chapter of Acts, Peter and John were arrested for proclaiming the gospel and were later released. The Scriptures tell us:

> On their release, Peter and John went back to their own people and reported all that the chief priests and the elders had said to them. When they heard this, they raised their voices together in prayer to God. "Sovereign Lord," they [began],

"you made the heaven and the earth and the sea, and every-thing in them." (Acts 4:23–24)

Jesus's disciples continued to pray, and the Lord answered them mightily. *"After they prayed, the place where they were meeting was shaken. And they were all filled with the Holy Spirit and spoke the word of God boldly"* (Acts 4:31).

Later, we see that the disciples continued to follow the lifestyle of prayer that Jesus had demonstrated for them. They declared, *"We…will give our attention to prayer and the ministry of the word"* (Acts 6:3–4). The entire book of Acts describes how they continued the ministry of Jesus through prayer and the power of the Holy Spirit. They learned the secret to Jesus's effectiveness in ministry. Now that you have learned the same secret, what will you do with it?

Let's pray together:

Heavenly Father,

Like Jesus's disciples, we, too, need to learn to pray. Thank You for giving us this model prayer so we can know how to pray as Jesus did and be effective in ministry, as He was. Your Word says, *"The one who calls you is faithful and he will do it"* (1 Thessalonians 5:24). You have called us to a lifestyle of prayer, and we ask You to fulfill that calling in us. Give us hearts to seek an intimate relationship with You every day and to follow Your thoughts and ways rather than our own thoughts and ways—or others' opinions. We pray this in the name of Jesus, our Great Intercessor. Amen.

Thought: The disciples continued to follow the lifestyle of prayer that Jesus had demonstrated for them.

Reading: Acts 4:23–37

— DAY 44 —

BECOME SILENT

"Be still, and know that I am God."   —Psalm 46:10

I want to show you a useful approach for organizing your steps in prayer. The "Twelve Action Steps in Prayer" that we will explore today and in upcoming devotions were developed from principles drawn from the prayer lives of Jesus, Abraham, Joseph, Moses, David, Ezekiel, and others in the Bible. When you study these biblical figures, you see that they all used a similar pattern in prayer. Their prayers received God's attention and produced powerful results. *"The prayer of a righteous man is powerful and effective"* (James 5:16).

The first step in prayer is to *become silent*. Prayer should begin with silence. We don't normally make a practice of being silent before God, but it's a very important aspect of prayer. To be silent means to gather oneself, to be still.

In Matthew 6:6, Jesus said, *"When you pray, go into your room, close the door and pray to your Father, who is unseen. Then your Father, who sees what is done in secret, will reward you."* Jesus was telling us to go to a quiet and private place where we will not be disturbed. In New Testament times, most of the roofs of the houses were flat, and people often prayed on the roof. That was their quiet place. They would go there to get away from all the noise and busyness in the house.

When you begin to enter into prayer, first get quiet and eliminate distractions. We are usually distracted by many things when we come to prayer. You can't pray effectively when all around you the children are playing, the television is blaring, and people are asking you questions. Prayer necessitates collecting yourself—your thoughts, your attention, your concentration. You need silence or isolation because you have to pull your entire self together.

Let the Lord calm your heart. *"You will keep in perfect peace him whose mind is steadfast, because he trusts in you"* (Isaiah 26:3). The word for *"peace"* in Hebrew is *shalom*, which means "more than enough." It means prosperity. Everything you need is provided in God, so you don't have to be distracted by worry when you pray.

Therefore, when you come before the Lord, in whatever private place you find to do so, get quiet and listen to nothing but God. Let your heart be restful, and come into the quiet place. That's when you are really praying. Too often, we try to rush this process. The Bible says, *"Be still, and know that I am God"* (Psalm 46:10).

I encourage you to spend time in quiet contemplation before the Lord. It's all right to say nothing. Many times, we start talking right away. Just become silent and bring your whole self to prayer. If you are trying to pray, but your spirit, body, mind, and emotions are separated, then you are not "one"—you are not unified. You will be unable to pray God's will with singleness of purpose. Silence helps bring you into a unity of heart and purpose with yourself and God.

⌒

Thought: Prayer necessitates collecting yourself and coming into a quiet place before God.

Reading: Psalm 37:5–7

— Day 45 —

OFFER ADORATION

"Yours, O Lord, is the greatness and the power and the glory and the majesty and the splendor, for everything in heaven and earth is yours." —1 Chronicles 29:11

The second step in prayer is to *offer adoration*. This step corresponds to hallowing God's name, mentioned in Jesus's model prayer. (See Luke 11:2.) Adoration means worshipping God. When you adore someone, you express how precious that person is to you. The first part of Psalm 95 is a good Scripture passage for this purpose. As a matter of fact, you could put your own tune to this psalm and sing it during the day:

> *Come, let us sing for joy to the Lord; let us shout aloud to the Rock of our salvation. Let us come before him with thanksgiving and extol him with music and song. For the Lord is the great God, the great King above all gods. In his hand are the depths of the earth, and the mountain peaks belong to him. The sea is his, for he made it, and his hands formed the dry land. Come, let us bow down in worship, let us kneel before the Lord our Maker; for he is our God and we are the people of his pasture, the flock under his care.* (Psalm 95:1–7)

What a song of adoration! *"Come, let us bow down in worship."* We are to worship God for who He is: King of all the earth, our Creator, our Savior, our All in All. *"Yours, O Lord, is the greatness and the power and the glory and the majesty and the splendor, for everything in heaven and earth is yours"* (1 Chronicles 29:11).

Start worshipping God. Start adoring Him. Start blessing Him. Start describing Him. Tell Him how you see Him.

You can say, "Lord, You are powerful, great, awesome, omnipotent, matchless. You are God above everyone and everything. You are merciful and wonderful. You are my Counselor. You are perfect. You are abiding. You are never weak. You are eternal. You are above all things and in all things. Everything receives its meaning in You, Lord. You are powerful. There is nothing besides You and no one who can compare with You. You alone are God. You are the only wise God: no one is as wise as You are. You are all-knowing: You know everything about me and everyone else. You understand things I don't understand. You are higher and deeper than my problems. I have no problems when You are present. You are all in all, and You are through all. Yes, Lord, there is no one like You!"

Thought: We are to worship God for who He is: King of all the earth, our Creator, our Savior, our All in All.

Reading: Psalm 150:1–6

MAKE CONFESSION

"If we confess our sins, he is faithful and just and will forgive us our sins and purify us from all unrighteousness."
—1 John 1:9

The third step in prayer is to *make confession*. Most of us have been taught that confession means bringing up our past sins, feeling remorse, getting emotional, and so on. That's not the heart of confession. Confession is a very different concept. It means agreeing with God about what He says *to* you and *about* you. You can agree with God only when you can hear what He is saying to you. This brings us back to adoration.

When you enter into God's presence through adoration, He is not going to start dealing with other people first. He's going to start shining His light on places you thought He never knew anything about. He's going to bring things into the open. God says to us, in effect, "I don't want you to condemn yourself; I want you to tell Me I'm right. Am I right? Is it sin? If it is, then you must agree with Me that it is wrong and stop doing it."

Thus, confession takes place when God points out something in your life and says, "Get rid of that," or "That's rebellion," or "That's sin," and you say, "Yes, God, You're right. I won't do that any longer." Then you put your trust in Him to enable you to walk by the Spirit. *"Live by the Spirit, and you will not gratify the desires of the sinful nature"* (Galatians 5:16). When the Holy Spirit shows you something in your life that is not right, then you are to agree with Him. If you disagree with Him, you're not confessing. This means unforgiven sin is sin that you never acknowledge as sin. You keep holding on to it and doing it; therefore, God cannot cleanse you from it. *"If we claim to be without sin, we deceive ourselves and the truth is not in us"* (1 John 1:8).

If you continue to play with sin and don't agree with God about it, it will destroy you. What you have been desiring in your life will never happen, for you will be the ruination of your own pursuits. Think about what God is saying. Confession doesn't involve merely bringing up your past. It involves agreeing with and obeying God immediately when He shows you that you are wrong. Then God will draw near to you.

If you ever find that you are wrong, just confess it, agree with God about it, ask for forgiveness, and go on with your life. Whatever wrongdoing you justify to yourself and others, you cannot repent of. Maybe you're justifying why you fell back into a certain sin. God asks you, "Is it sin?" Just answer, "Yes, God, forgive me. I was wrong. I'm back home." "Good. You agree with Me that it's sin; now, I will forgive you. I will cleanse you from all unrighteousness. Let Me clean you up."

God is faithful. Once He cleanses you, there isn't anyone who can condemn you. *"Who will bring any charge against those whom God has chosen? It is God who justifies. Who is he that condemns?"* (Romans 8:33–34).

⌒

Thought: Confession means agreeing with God about what He says *to* you and *about* you.

Reading: Psalm 51:1–12

103

GIVE THANKS AND MAKE SUPPLICATION

"Give thanks to the LORD, for he is good; his love endures forever." —1 Chronicles 16:34

Step four in prayer is to *give thanks*. *"Be joyful always; pray continually; give thanks in all circumstances, for this is God's will for you in Christ Jesus"* (1 Thessalonians 5:16–18).

Thanksgiving is God's will for us. After you have confessed, start giving thanks. Of course, now that you've confessed, you can give thanks abundantly because your heart is free. God has not only given you freedom, but He has also given you something to be thankful for. He has just forgiven you of your sin. You have enough to be thankful for to last hours!

David was thinking of thanksgiving even as he confessed his great sin to God. *"Save me from bloodguilt, O God, the God who saves me, and my tongue will sing of your righteousness. O Lord, open my lips, and my mouth will declare your praise"* (Psalm 51:14–15). That's the way to pray. As a matter of fact, this confession psalm ends in worship. *"The sacrifices of God are a broken spirit; a broken and contrite heart, O God, you will not despise…. Then there will be righteous sacrifices, whole burnt offerings to delight you; then bulls will be offered on your altar"* (verses 17, 19). Offering sacrifices and burnt offerings was an Old Testament method of worship. If you have confessed before God, then your heart is right, and you can offer sacrifices of praise to God. (See Hebrews 13:15.)

We can always be thankful for and praise God for the gift of salvation in Jesus Christ. *"Come, let us sing for joy to the LORD; let us shout aloud to the Rock of our salvation. Let us come before him with thanksgiving and extol him with music and song"* (Psalm 95:1–2).

After giving thanks, the next step in prayer is to *make suppli-cation*. Philippians 4:6 says, *"Do not be anxious about anything, but in everything, by prayer and petition [*"supplication"* KJV, NKJV], with thanksgiving, present your requests to God."*

"Supplication" is a word that implies three things: interceding, petitioning, and brooding. By "brooding," I mean having a deep passion. When you offer supplication, it means you feel the heart of God. You desire His will so much that it becomes an emotional experience. This is usually when you begin to weep in prayer or pray more fervently. It's an emotionally overwhelming experience of God. God shows you some of what He's feeling, and you become unified with His purposes and desires.

Supplication is a natural outgrowth of thanksgiving. When you give thanks, you usually move into supplication because thanksgiving pleases God, and He reveals to you what is in His heart.

$\sim$

Thought: Supplication is a natural outgrowth of thanksgiving.

Reading: Psalm 136

—DAY 48—
SPECIFY PETITIONS AND REQUESTS

*"In every situation, by prayer and petition, with thanksgiving,
present your requests to God."* —Philippians 4:6 (NIV2011)

The sixth step in prayer is to *specify your petitions and requests.*
Prayer is not just mumbo jumbo. It is a very articulate, intentional
communication. It is an art. A lawyer does much studying before
he stands before a judge and jury to present his case. That's what
he is paid to do. He does his research so he can bring informa-
tion pertinent to the case. A common thing you hear a prosecutor
or defense lawyer say is, "Irrelevant!" Similarly, when you come
before God to petition for things that you want Him to do, you
have to be sure the evidence you bring is relevant to the case. This
is why God has so many names. You need to address Him specifically for your particular petitions.

If you want peace, you appeal to Him as Jehovah-Shalom
(The Lord our Peace), rather than Jehovah-Jireh (The Lord our
Provider). If you need healing, He is Jehovah-Rapha (The Lord
our Healer). "Lord, I need You to be Jehovah-Rapha specifically in
this case. I am appealing to the court for healing. I don't need a car
right now; I can't even drive it. I need to be healed. You say that if I
love You and follow Your commands, *'the* LORD *will take away from*
[me] *all sickness'* (Deuteronomy 7:15 NKJV)."

Therefore, specify your petitions by acknowledging God's
name and Word. One way to do this is to write down the things
you want to pray for; next to those items, write down the Scriptures
that you're going to use when you pray. Again, prayer needs to be
intentional and practical. It's not something you throw together.
It's good to have things written down specifically. Then, when

you pray about your list of petitions, God will know that there is thought and intention behind your requests. When you pray for each request, you are praying according to God's Word, and God will send help for each request. *"This is the confidence we have in approaching God: that if we ask anything **according to his will**, he hears us. And if we know that he hears us—whatever we ask—we know that we have what we asked of him"* (1 John 5:14–15).

In the Scriptures, the apostle Paul directed us that *"in every situation,"* we are to bring our requests before God: *"Do not be anxious about anything, but in every situation, by prayer and petition, with thanksgiving, present your requests to God. And the peace of God, which transcends all understanding, will guard your hearts and your minds in Christ Jesus"* (Philippians 4:6–7 NIV2011). So, be specific and Scripture-based in your prayers. God will hear you.

⌣⌐

Thought: Prayer needs to be intentional and practical.

Reading: Matthew 20:30–34

— DAY 49 —

SECURE THE PROMISES

"For no matter how many promises God has made, they are 'Yes' in Christ. And so through him the 'Amen' is spoken by us to the glory of God."   —2 Corinthians 1:20

The seventh step in prayer is to *secure the promises*. Hold on to God's promises as you take His Word before Him, applying it to the particular request you are making.

When Jesus wanted to minister to people, He never assumed what they needed. He would ask them, *"What do you want me to do for you?"* (Matthew 20:32). Again, God answers specific requests based on His promises. Let's look at an example of this.

Bartimaeus was blind, and he was begging by the side of the road. *"When he heard that it was Jesus of Nazareth, he began to shout, 'Jesus, Son of David, have mercy on me!'"* (Mark 10:47). Jesus inquired of him, *"What do you want me to do for you?"* (verse 51). You might think that would have been obvious, but Jesus had people tell Him what they specifically wanted. *"The blind man said, 'Rabbi, I want to see.' 'Go,' said Jesus, 'your faith has healed you.' Immediately he received his sight and followed Jesus along the road"* (verses 51–52).

Bartimaeus was healed because he asked for healing based on his legal rights. He was crying out, *"Son of David"* (Mark 10:47, 48). Abraham's covenant came through David. Scripture says the Messiah will come through David's line and that David's throne will last forever. (See Isaiah 9:6–7.) Bartimaeus reasoned, "If Jesus is the Messiah, He must be the Son of David. If He is the Son of David, then every covenant promise God made to Abraham, Moses, and David can come to me through Him." So, he said, 'Son *of David, have mercy on me!'* (Mark 10:47, 48). "'Go,' *said Jesus, 'your faith has healed you'"* (verse 52). The man deserved healing because he petitioned specifically through the promises. Likewise, we are to secure the promises when we pray.

Now let's look at another biblical example. In this case, although the woman involved didn't ask Jesus for healing, she was still healed based on the promises. One Sabbath day, Jesus walked into a synagogue and saw this woman, who was hunched over and couldn't lift herself up. Jesus spoke a word of healing, put His hands on her, and healed her. *"Immediately she straightened up and praised God"* (Luke 13:13).

The religious leaders began to murmur, "How dare He heal her on the Sabbath day!" Jesus turned to them and said, *"Should not this woman, **a daughter of Abraham**, whom Satan has kept bound for eighteen long years, be set free on the Sabbath day from what bound her?"* (Luke 13:16).

That was a powerful statement. Jesus healed her because, in the contract God had made with His chosen people on behalf of Abraham, He had said, *"The* Lord *will take away from you all sickness"* (Deuteronomy 7:15 kjv, nkjv).

We often ask the Lord to heal us because we're hurting, and He does have compassion on us to heal us. (See, for example, Matthew 14:14.) However, the primary reason He heals us is that we give Him evidence that healing is our legal right.

⌒

Thought: When you petition the Lord, take God's promises before Him, applying them to the specific request you are making. Then hold on to God's promises.

Reading: 2 Peter 1:3–4

— DAY 50 —

PLEAD YOUR CASE

"Will not God bring about justice for his chosen ones, who cry out to him day and night?"   —Luke 18:7

The eighth step in prayer is to *plead your case*. Pleading your case does not mean begging and moaning before God and becoming emotional. It is something you do because you rightfully deserve what you are asking for based on God's promises.

In Luke 18, through a parable, Jesus revealed to His disciples how to go all the way in prayer until we see God. He began by saying, *"In a certain town there was a judge who neither feared God nor cared about men"* (verse 2). I think Jesus used the example of the worst possible judge to illustrate the fact that prayer doesn't have anything to do with God liking you. We say, "Lord, if You love me, bless me." God answers, "I bless you because of two things: first, you qualify through faith in My promises and righteous living; and, second, I am holy; therefore, I keep My Word."

Jesus continued, *"And there was a widow in that town who kept coming to him with the plea, 'Grant me justice against my adversary'"* (verse 3). The reason He used the illustration of a widow is that, in Jesus's day, a widow was someone who had really hit rock-bottom in life. Often, there were no relatives to care for her and help her. The widow is important to this example because God wants you to come to prayer with an attitude that says, "You're the only One who can help me." He wants us to depend completely on Him.

Jesus went on to say, *"For some time [the judge] refused"* (Luke 18:4). Again, when we pray, sometimes the answer doesn't come right away, but that doesn't mean it's not on the way. Jesus concluded His story with this statement: *"Finally [the judge] said to* himself, 'Even though I don't fear God or care about men, yet because this widow keeps bothering me, I will see that she gets justice, so that she won't eventually wear me out with her coming!'" (Luke 18:4–5).

Here is how Jesus explained the parable to His disciples: "*Listen to what the unjust judge says. And will not God bring about justice for his* **chosen ones**, *who cry out to him day and night? Will he keep putting them off? I tell you, he will see that they get justice, and quickly*" (verses 6–8). Jesus was saying, "If a man who doesn't acknowledge God or His righteousness has to see to it that a woman he doesn't like gets what she deserves, how much more will God, who loves you, see to it that you get justice—and quickly?" In other words, God isn't going to take as long as that judge who didn't like people. He will give justice to His chosen ones, those who have received His promises as a spiritual inheritance.

This parable assures us that when we believe God's Word and repeat His promises back to Him, God says, "I'm going to answer you—not because I 'like' you but because I am holy." Therefore, plead your case based on God's Word and integrity.

⌒

Thought: God will give justice to His chosen ones, those who have received His promises as a spiritual inheritance.

Reading: Isaiah 30:18

— DAY 51 —

BELIEVE

*"Therefore I tell you, whatever you ask for in prayer, believe
that you have received it, and it will be yours."*—Mark 11:24

Step nine in prayer is to *believe*. This is a difficult step for many
of us. As in the parable of the unjust judge we looked at in the
previous devotion, God says that after we plead our case, we are
to believe. (See Luke 18:8.) Asking, in itself, doesn't cause us to
receive.

Read carefully the words of Christ in this passage from Mark
11. This is another mini-seminar on prayer:

*"Have faith in God," Jesus answered. "I tell you the truth,
if anyone says to this mountain, 'Go, throw yourself into the
sea,' and does not doubt in his heart but believes that what he
says will happen, it will be done for him. Therefore I tell you,
whatever you ask for in prayer, believe...."* (verses 22–24)

What's the next phrase? *"...that you have received it."* Do you
see the *"-ed"* in *"received"*? When you ask, believe right then and
there that you have already received it. It is possible to ask for
something in prayer and not believe. We do it all the time. We
usually give up too soon.

In the book of Daniel, we read that Daniel prayed and that, the
same day he prayed, the answer was on its way. However, Daniel
didn't know that. (See Daniel 10:10–14; see also Daniel 9:23).
What did Daniel do? He kept praying. After twenty-one days,
an angel arrived with the answer. The point is, Daniel didn't say,
"Well, it's been ten days now. This thing doesn't work. I'm going
back to doing what I had been doing." No. Daniel believed that if

God said something, it was supposed to happen. He wasn't going to stop praying until it was manifested. He was going to persevere until he saw it with his own eyes.

Do you believe that what you prayed for last night is going to happen? I want you to confess something. Say, "Lord, I believe." You might not be a believer all the way. Maybe you tend to doubt. When you start doubting, though, be honest, like the father of the demon-possessed boy, and say, "Lord, I believe; help my unbelief!" (Mark 9:24 NKJV). That's a good prayer. We can't let doubt enter into our prayers. It will short-circuit them.

> If any of you lacks wisdom, he should ask God, who gives generously to all without finding fault, and it will be given to him. But when he asks, he must believe and not doubt, because he who doubts is like a wave of the sea, blown and tossed by the wind. That man should not think he will receive anything from the Lord. (James 1:5–7)

Instead of being like the person who doubts, "tossed by the wind," believe that you have received what you asked for, and it will be yours.

⸻

Thought: When you ask for something in prayer, believe right then and there that you have already received it.

Reading: Ephesians 1:18–21

GIVE THANKS AGAIN

"It is good to give thanks to the LORD, and to sing praises to Your name, O Most High."   —Psalm 92:1 (NKJV)

The tenth step in prayer is to *give thanks*. You might say, "But 'give thanks' was step four." However, there is a progression in prayer. After you have believed, offer thanksgiving again!

Let's compare the two thanksgivings in prayer. The first thanksgiving expresses your appreciation for God's forgiveness and mercy. The second thanksgiving is the highest form of faith. You thank God for what you don't yet see because you believe it is already done. That takes faith. If you truly believe that when you prayed, you received what you asked for, then you will start thanking Him. We are not to wait until we see the manifestation of our answers before expressing our gratitude.

In fact, we don't show God that we really believe until we thank Him. We do this for humans, but we don't do it for God. For instance, suppose you go to the bank and talk to the manager about getting a loan. The banker approves the loan and says, "Consider it done. The money will be deposited into your account." You don't see the money. You don't know if he has already deposited the money or not. Yet what do you say? "Thank you very much." Then you go and do your business based on the banker's word. God says, "Do the same for Me. Thank Me before it is even registered on your account statement." Why? If we will believe God, then the answer will come.

Oftentimes, we block the answers to our prayers. The answer was coming, but we walked away, saying, "I'm not wasting my time believing that anymore." What happens then? Remember the passage from James 1 that we read yesterday? *"He who doubts is like a wave of the sea, blown and tossed by the wind. That man should not think he will receive anything from the Lord"* (James 1:6–7).

Don't block your prayers. Start giving thanks, and thank God until the answer manifests itself.

If someone asks you, "How are you doing?" just say, "I'm thanking God for what I have received." If you are asked, "How are you feeling?" say, "I'm feeling really good." "Why?" "I'm thanking God for what is going to be manifested." When you respond like that, you start attracting angels. The Bible says, *"Are not all angels ministering spirits sent to serve those who will inherit salvation?"* (Hebrews 1:14).

You can close all your prayer times with thanksgiving because you have already received what you have asked for. It just hasn't been revealed yet for other people to see!

> *Enter his gates with thanksgiving and his courts with praise; give thanks to him and praise his name. For the* Lord *is good and his love endures forever; his faithfulness continues through all generations.* (Psalm 100:4–5)

Thought: If you truly believe that when you prayed, you received what you asked for, then you will start thanking Him.

Reading: Colossians 2:6–7

—DAY 53—

LIVE IN EXPECTATION

*"Now to him who is able to do immeasurably more than all we
ask or imagine, according to his power that is at work within
us."*   —Ephesians 3:20

The eleventh step in prayer is to *live in expectation*. Continue in
a spirit of thanksgiving by living in expectation of the answer to
your prayer.

My life has changed as I have personally applied this principle.
More and more, as I have walked with the Lord, He has taught me
foundational truths that have made a significant difference in my
life.

If you believe you are going to be blessed financially, if you
expect God to bless you, then I suggest you do something similar
to what I did. Several years ago, I said to my banker, "I want to
open a new account." He asked, "For what?" I said, "For something
I expect." I have several different accounts in that bank, but I said,
"This one is different. This is my blessing account. I'm expecting
God to bless me, and I'm going to prove to Him that I expect it by
actually giving Him somewhere to put it. If I put it in my check-
ing account, I might not keep it. If I put it in the loan account, it
might get lost. I'm going to give God a target where He can aim the
blessings." After I opened that account, I had more money in my
life than ever before.

Many times, people come to me and say, "Pastor Myles, I'm
praying for a job." I say, "How many applications have you filled
out?" "Well, I'm waiting for the Lord to lead me to something." Of
course, we need to follow God's leading, but too often we're lazy
and don't believe. We need to knock. If you believe that God will

give you a job, then fill out every application you can because God is going to bring one of them to you. If the employer doesn't know you're there, how can he call you for an interview?

Live in expectation! If you ask God to provide you with a car so you can drive to church to worship Him, and you believe God heard you, then go shopping. Don't go back to church saying, "Well, the Lord will arrange it." Go to the car lot and look around. Why? You expect God to do something. Perhaps you are praying for a spouse. Look your best. That person might show up today. If you don't expect, that means you don't believe. Make arrangements for your answer! *"Now to him who is able to do immeasurably more than all we ask or imagine, according to his power that is at work within us"* (Ephesians 3:20).

⌒

Thought: Continue in a spirit of thanksgiving by living in expectation of the answer to your prayer.

Reading: Psalm 147:7–11

— Day 54 —

PRACTICE ACTIVE BELIEF

"Ask and it will be given to you; seek and you will find; knock and the door will be opened to you." —Luke 11:9

The twelfth and final step in prayer is to *practice active belief.* This shows you are living in expectation. It is what Jesus meant by "seeking and knocking." We know that when the disciples asked, *"Lord, teach us to pray"* (Luke 11:1), Jesus proceeded to teach them a model prayer. Luke 11:9 is part of His discourse on prayer: *"So I say to you: Ask and it will be given to you; seek and you will find; knock and the door will be opened to you."*

Jesus is telling us, "Don't stop after you pray. Get up and go look for what you asked for. You will find it if you seek it. It may be behind some closed doors. If that is the case, then knock." If you believe it is yours, or it is supposed to be yours, or it is rightfully yours in Christ, no door or barrier can stop what God has for you. When the devil tries to hold it back, just keep persisting until the door falls down. According to the Word of God, if you knock, it will come to pass. This is the meaning of active prayer.

Again, if you are believing God for a new house, then go looking. Drive around the neighborhoods that have the kind of house you want. Use your faith in proportion to your confession. Say, "God, I believe You for this." Then go seeking. Call realtors and ask, "What do you have on the market?" Ask people who live in the area that you like to let you know about any of their neighbors who might be putting their houses on the market. In this way, you can practice active belief as you continue to live before God in holiness and truth. God will bless you when you ask, seek, and knock.

As you learn how to pray according to biblical principles, you will become a powerfully effective believer. Use these twelve action steps as a guide to prayer, and make sure everything in your life is in order according to God's will and purposes. I'm excited about what God is going to do in your life as you apply these principles and as you grow in the grace and knowledge of God and His ways!

Let's pray together:

Heavenly Father,

Thank You for giving us principles for prayer in Your Word. Psalm 119:15 says, "*I meditate on your precepts and consider your ways.*" Don't allow us to walk away from Your truths and forget them. Help us to study Your principles and consider carefully Your ways as revealed in Your Word. Then encourage us to step out in faith to put these principles into practice in our lives. As we do, we thank You for answering our prayers and doing "*immeasurably more than all we ask or imagine, according to* [Your] *power that is at work within us*" (Ephesians 3:20). We pray this in the name of Jesus, the Mediator of the new covenant. Amen.

Thought: Don't stop after you have prayed. Get up and seek what you have asked for. If you seek and knock, it will come to pass.

Reading: Hebrews 10:36–39

— DAY 55 —

LEARNING ABOUT PRAYER BUT NOT PRACTICING IT

"Do not merely listen to the word, and so deceive yourselves. Do what it says."   —James 1:22

Prayer is the greatest opportunity and privilege offered to a person in Christ. Yet because of the power of prayer, our adversary, Satan, makes it his business to see that the prayers of individuals and churches are ineffective. He will use misconceptions about prayer to thwart our prayer potential. These misconceptions are *hurdles* to overcome as we address the various problems that lead to unanswered prayer. Rising above these hurdles through God's grace will enable you to truly understand the purpose and power of prayer. In the next several devotions, we will address six such hurdles.

The first hurdle is a desire to just *read about* the Bible and prayer rather than to *study* the Word itself and *equip oneself* for prayer. We gain a false sense of satisfaction when we learn about something but don't actually do anything with it. We think it's a part of our lives, but it hasn't made it from our heads to our hearts, from theory to practice.

Satan loves it when we read about what we should be doing but never do it; when we purchase books on prayer and the Bible but never follow what the books say; when we buy recordings of Bible teachings but never practice what the teachings instruct us to do. Many Christians read in the Bible about how believers received answers to their prayers, and they feel inspired. They may say, "Daniel prayed, Joseph prayed, and look at the results they had. *'The prayer of a righteous man is powerful and effective'* (James 5:16).

I should pray too." However, they never make the commitment to do it.

We often have the erroneous idea that if we *know* a great deal about prayer, somehow we *have* prayed. A major cause of unanswered prayer is our becoming experts in the knowledge of prayer but not masters in the practice of praying. The best approach to prayer is *to pray*.

The second hurdle to prayer is similar to the first: *mental assent rather than action*. Mental assent looks so much like faith that many people cannot see the difference between the two. Mental assent means intellectually accepting the Word as true—admiring it and agreeing with it—but not allowing it to have an impact on you, so that it doesn't do you any good. In essence, mental assent *agrees with* God but does not *believe* God. The mental assentor affirms that the entire Bible came from God and that *every* word of it is true. When a crisis comes, however, they say, "Yes, I believe the Bible is true, but it doesn't work for *me*."

If you have been mentally assenting to the truth but not acting on it, you have been living below your privilege for too long. James 1:22 says, *"Do not merely listen to the word, and so deceive yourselves. Do what it says."* This verse separates mental assent from faith. We have to live out our faith by doing what God asks. We should not only agree with His Word and will but also live them.

⌒

Thought: The only way God's promises will become a reality in your life is for you to act on them—and you can't act on them without faith.

Reading: Matthew 7:24–27

HEARING THE WORD BUT
NOT ABSORBING IT

"He who has ears to hear, let him hear!"
—Matthew 13:9 (NKJV)

The third major hurdle to answered prayer is *hearing the Word but not absorbing it* into one's life. Skipping the step of absorbing the Word is detrimental to our spiritual health because we must internalize the Word if it is going to make a difference in our lives. When we don't absorb the Word, it often goes in one ear and out the other. Satan steals it away so that it can't have an impact on our relationship with God.

In the parable of the sower, Jesus said, *"When anyone hears the message about the kingdom and does not understand it, the evil one comes and snatches away what was sown in his heart"* (Matthew 13:19). In this parable, the Word of God is depicted as seed, while various types of human attitudes are represented by different types of soil. When the seed is sown along the path—that is, when the Word does not become a central part of a person's life—the enemy comes *immediately* to steal it. In his attempt to destroy the work of God in our lives, Satan's first target is the source of our spiritual life—the Word. This means that even as you are reading this book, the enemy is trying to steal God's truth from you.

Jesus often ended His teachings by saying, *"He who has ears to hear, let him hear!"* (See, for example, Matthew 13:9 NKJV; Luke 14:35 NKJV.) There is physical hearing, and there is spiritual hearing. Jesus knew that the people were listening to His words. However, He told them, in essence, "My words need to become established in your hearts."

I like how *The Living Bible* paraphrases Jesus's command in Revelation 2:7: *"Let this message sink into the ears of anyone who listens to what the Spirit is saying to the churches."* Let the message sink in. Stay focused after you've heard or read the Word, and let it truly sink into your spirit. The Bible calls this process *meditation*. Biblical meditation in very different from transcendental meditation, practiced in Far Eastern religions. Transcendental meditation involves chanting and incantation, while biblical meditation focuses solely on God's Word.

After the apostle Paul instructed Timothy in God's ways, he said, *"Meditate on these things; give yourself entirely to them, that your progress may be evident to all"* (1 Timothy 4:15 NKJV). The Greek word for *"meditate"* in this verse is *meletao*, which means "to revolve in the mind." Again, biblical mediation is not a mindless process of chanting but of *using* your mind—mentally turning something over and over in order to understand all its truths and implications, and then embracing those truths by applying them to your whole life.

Satan never wants you to get to the meditation stage because that is when the Word of God can become the means for answered prayer. If Satan can steal the Word from you, he can steal what God has given you to fulfill His purposes in your life.

⌒

Thought: Stay focused after you've heard or read the Word, and let it truly sink into your spirit.

Reading: James 1:23–25

"HOPING" RATHER THAN HAVING FAITH

"A righteousness that is by faith from first to last, just as it is written: 'The righteous will live by faith.'" —Romans 1:17

Another common hurdle that blocks people's prayers is *"hoping" rather than having faith.* There are two ways in which the idea of hope can interfere with what God wants to accomplish through prayer: (1) when we apply the biblical definition of hope (future fulfillment) to present-day faith situations, and (2) when our hope is not the biblical kind but is really just wishful thinking.

First, many people mistake hope for faith. The Bible says, *"And now these three remain: faith, hope and love. But the greatest of these is love"* (1 Corinthians 13:13). Remember that the Greek word for *"faith"* is *pistis*, meaning "belief" or "confidence." It can also mean "conviction" or "assurance." The word for *"hope"* is *elpis*, meaning "expectation" or "confidence." Biblical hope is based on faith because hope is the confident anticipation of the fulfillment of that faith.

Hope is a beautiful and necessary thing when it is about heaven, the second coming of Christ, and everything God has promised us in the future—the culmination of our salvation, the resurrection of our bodies, the new heaven and earth, and our reigning with Jesus forever. The assurance of future blessings is what biblical hope is all about: *"We have this hope as an anchor for the soul, firm and secure"* (Hebrews 6:19). However, this kind of hope can become a hurdle to answered prayer when it is misapplied. There are blessings God wants to give us in the present day. If we think they are all in the future, we will not exercise our faith to see their fulfillment in our lives *now.* Believers who have this perspective will receive the future blessings for which they have faith and hope, but they will miss out on the blessings God wants to give them today.

Second, there is a type of hope that is really just *wishful thinking*. It is not based on faith, as biblical hope is. Instead, it is based on uncertainty or doubt. Think of the difference in this way: the first is hope; the second is "hoping." Hoping is when we say, "I hope this happens," or "I hope this works," or "I hope God hears my prayers."

Hebrews 11:1 declares, "*Now faith is being **sure** of what we hope for and **certain** of what we do not see*." "Hoping" is dangerous because it can cancel our prayers. Suppose you ask God for something according to His Word, and you say, "Lord, I believe." Then you get up from your prayer time and say, "Well, I hope it happens." You have just nullified your prayer.

How long have you been hoping to go to school, open a business, develop a skill, or lose weight? Perhaps two years, five years, ten years—and you still haven't done it. Hoping won't get anything accomplished. When we exhibit wishful thinking and doubt, we show that we don't really trust God, that we don't believe Him, that we are skeptical about His character and integrity.

God's blessings have already been accomplished in the spiritual realm. He is waiting for you to believe Him so He can release them!

⌒

Thought: Wishful thinking is a destructive element in the present-tense life and practice of prayer.

Reading: Mark 9:14–29

PRAYING FOR FAITH AND NEGLECTING PRAYER

"Faith comes from hearing the message, and the message is heard through the word of Christ." —Romans 10:17

The fifth common hurdle to answered prayer is *praying for faith.* Luke 17:5 says, *"The apostles said to the Lord, 'Increase our faith!'"* Have you ever prayed a prayer like that? You are in good company. The disciples lived with Jesus for over three years. They saw Him cast out demons, heal the sick, and raise the dead, yet they still implored Him, *"Increase our faith!"* His answer is wonderful: *"If you have faith as small as a mustard seed, you can say to this mulberry tree, 'Be uprooted and planted in the sea,' and it will obey you"* (verse 6).

Remember, our faith grows as the Word is taken into our lives and acted upon. Romans 10:17 says, *"Faith comes from hearing the message, and the message is heard through the word of Christ."* Faith comes and increases as we hear and believe the Word and put it into practice.

It is not the size of your faith that counts—it is the size of your God. If you want to increase your faith, it will not come from praying for it; it will come when you increase your intake of the Word of God. What you know of the Word becomes the limit of your faith because you can believe only what you know.

Let's now look at one final hurdle to prayer that we need to recognize: *neglecting prayer altogether,* either through sheer laziness or because of life's busyness and distractions. Laziness and neglect are the worst reasons for not praying. None of us wants to be called a *"wicked, lazy servant"* (Matthew 25:26) by God in regard to this crucial purpose for our lives.

In the parable of the sower, Jesus spoke about distractions that can pull us away from our most important priorities in life: *"The one who received the seed that fell among the thorns is the man who hears the word, but the worries of this life and the deceitfulness of wealth choke it, making it unfruitful"* (Matthew 13:22). When a person doesn't want to bother with prayer because they feel they have more important things to do, or when they allow the many concerns of this life to crowd out the practice of prayer, then whatever they do know about prayer will not bear any fruit in their life.

As we conclude these devotions on the hurdles to prayer, I encourage you to identify at least one hurdle that represents your current practice of prayer. Then, consciously take steps to correct it by applying the truth of God's Word to it.

Let's pray together:

Heavenly Father,

We ask You to help us remain alert to the hurdles in our lives that the enemy wants to use to destroy our prayer potential. Help us to resist him as we stand firm in our faith. Let Your Holy Spirit show us where we are being deceived in our attitudes toward prayer and the Word so we can understand and practice true and effective prayer. We ask these things in the name of Jesus, who resisted the enemy through the power of Your Word. Amen.

Thought: Faith comes and increases as we hear and believe the Word and put it into practice.

Reading: Mark 4:13–20

SIN AND FEAR

"If I regard iniquity in my heart, the Lord will not hear me."
—Psalm 66:18 (KJV)

In addition to hurdles to prayer, there are spiritual and emotional *hindrances to prayer*. We must address these hindrances if we are to have true fellowship with God and receive answers to our prayers. Clearing out hindrances in our lives will enable us to live in harmony with God and others and to have confidence in prayer. Although some of these hindrances were mentioned in earlier devotions, it will be helpful to review them together over the next several days.

First, we must acknowledge *the impact of sin* in our lives and the ways in which it hinders us. Sin, as the Bible says, *"is so prevalent"* (James 1:21), and our fallen nature causes many problems and misunderstandings in regard to our faith, obedience, and prayers. When there is sin—especially willful sin—in your life, and you are not obeying the Word, God will not hear you. You will not receive His favor. Isaiah 59:2 tells us, *"Your iniquities have separated you from your God; your sins have hidden his face from you, so that he will not hear."* However, when we sin, 1 John 2:1 assures us, *"If anybody does sin, we have one who speaks to the Father in our defense—Jesus Christ, the Righteous One."* We can be forgiven and restored to right relationship with God through Christ.

Fear is a second significant hindrance for us to overcome because it often keeps us from believing we can go to God in prayer. First John 4:18 says, *"There is no fear in love. But perfect love drives out fear, because fear has to do with punishment [*"because fear involves torment"* NKJV]. The one who fears is not made perfect* in love." The idea of *"punishment"* in this verse refers to our being afraid to approach God because we think He might remember a sin or failure on our part. We're afraid to ask God for anything because we believe He has something against us. It hinders us from having freedom and confidence when we pray. This kind of fear will block our faith, and, thus, our prayers will be ineffective.

The Bible says that *"fear involves torment."* Fear immobilizes you. It drains the energy from your body. It is worry without profit. It is faith in what could go wrong rather than faith in what could go right. It is believing what the devil is telling you and what other people are telling you rather than what God is saying to you.

When you go before God, it doesn't matter what your past was like, what you did yesterday, or even what you did this morning that was unpleasing to Him. If you confess your sin before God, appropriating the cleansing blood of Jesus to purify you from all unrighteousness (see 1 John 1:9), then He will forgive you, and you can approach Him as if you had never sinned. No fear needs to be involved in your prayers.

Be encouraged! God wants you to live with the assurance of forgiveness and to move forward in His purposes with confidence.

⟿

Thought: Clearing out hindrances in our lives will enable us to live in harmony with God and others and to have confidence in prayer.

Reading: Hebrews 4:14–16

— Day 60 —
GUILT

"Therefore, there is now no condemnation for those who are in Christ Jesus."   —Romans 8:1

Another significant hindrance to prayer is *guilt.* Guilt is related to the fear of not being forgiven. Some people live with a constant sense of being condemned by God; therefore, they always feel guilty. Thankfully, Romans 8:1–2 tells us, *"Therefore, there is now no condemnation for those who are in Christ Jesus, because through Christ Jesus the law of the Spirit of life set me free from the law of sin and* [its consequence] *death."*

"There is now no condemnation." This truth is crucial for us to understand if we are to approach God in prayer. I remember speaking at a prayer meeting about the freedom from condemnation that we have in Christ. After the meeting, someone came up to me and said, "That word was so important for me. I thought that because I'd done some terrible things in my life, God wasn't going to use me anymore. I felt as if God wouldn't want me to be a part of His work any longer. I asked for forgiveness, but I just needed to hear God say, 'It's okay. You're forgiven.'"

God has forgiven and forgotten your sin if you have confessed it, repented of it, and believed that it is covered by the blood of Jesus. Hebrews 8:12 records the Lord as saying, *"For I will forgive their wickedness and will remember their sins no more."*

Why do we struggle with guilt? Sometimes guilt comes from distrust. If you have asked God to forgive you, He has forgiven you. If you are still carrying the sin around in your heart and mind, then you are doubting that God forgave you. That is why the guilt comes back to life. The devil uses that guilt to undermine your faith; when you pray, your faith is weak, and so your prayers aren't answered.

The Lord says, "*I, even I, am he who blots out your transgressions, for my own sake, and remembers your sins no more*" (Isaiah 43:25). God chooses not to remember your sins once they have been forgiven. He does not allow them to stand in the way of your relationship with Him. One of my college professors used to say, "After we ask for forgiveness, God puts up a little sign that says, 'No fishing.'" God has cast your sins into the sea of forgetfulness. (See Micah 7:19.) Here's what's important about this fact: since God has chosen to forget them, He doesn't want you to remind Him about them, either!

If you are burdened with guilt about your past, you can walk into God's presence without feeling condemned. There is no condemnation for those who are in Christ Jesus because God has forgiven you through Christ. If you have sin in your life right now, put it under the blood of Jesus. Let Him cast your sin in the sea of forgetfulness so you can have power in prayer with God.

~

Thought: Accept God's forgiveness and draw near to Him again in confident faith.

Reading: Micah 7:19

— Day 61 —

FEELINGS OF INFERIORITY

"In love [God] predestined us to be adopted as his sons through Jesus Christ, in accordance with his pleasure and will."

—Ephesians 1:4–5

Feelings of inferiority will also impede the effectiveness of prayer. The way people feel about themselves plays a significant role in how they approach God. Some people don't believe they are worthy to receive answers to their prayers. When you have a low opinion of yourself, it is because you do not know God's true opinion of you, which He reveals in His Word. If that is how you feel, this is a crucial hurdle to overcome so that it will not sabotage your prayer life. You cannot pray effectively if you are ashamed of yourself and do not think you deserve to receive what you are asking God for.

The first chapter of Ephesians is a marvelous passage that describes how God truly feels about us. It was a special blessing to me when I was a teenager.

> *In love [God] **predestined us to be adopted as his sons** through Jesus Christ, in accordance with his pleasure and will—to the praise of his glorious grace, which he has freely given us in the One he loves. In him we have redemption through his blood, the forgiveness of sins, in accordance with the riches of God's grace that he lavished on us with all wisdom and understanding. And he made known to us the mystery of his will according to his good pleasure, which he purposed in Christ, to be put into effect when the times will have reached their fulfillment—to bring all things in heaven and on earth together under one head, even Christ. In him we were also **chosen**.*
>
> (Ephesians 1:4–11)

You were chosen in Christ long before the earth was made. God loves you so much that He has lavished His love on you. A low opinion of yourself or self-hatred is not from God but from the enemy. He doesn't want you to realize that if God loved you so much that He gave you the best He had, then your value to Him must be incalculable.

When you have the right estimation of yourself as a redeemed child of God, you don't come to prayer as someone who is begging. Instead, you confidently present your case. Prayer is not trying to get God to do something for you by making Him feel sorry for you. It is coming to Him knowing that you not only deserve what you ask because of the righteousness of Christ, but you also have a right to it because it is based on His Word.

We are God's own children, and we need to approach Him as His children. *"He made us accepted in the Beloved"* (Ephesians 1:6 NKJV). Remember, God loved you before the foundation of the earth. When you were estranged from Him by sin, He sent His Son to die for you. He has made you worthy in Christ Jesus. He has made you a coheir with His Son. Therefore, live and pray accordingly.

⌒

Thought: You can't *be* who you are if you don't *know* who you are. You are God's own child.

Reading: Ephesians 2:4–7

— Day 62 —

DOUBT AND WRONG MOTIVES

*"Let him ask in faith, with no doubting.... You ask and do not
receive, because you ask amiss ["because you ask with wrong
motives" NIV], that you may spend it on your pleasures."*
                                                    —James 1:6; 4:3 (NKJV)

Doubt is another major hindrance to answered prayer. Let's
review the following passage from the book of James:

> *If any of you lacks wisdom, he should ask God, who gives
> generously to all without finding fault, and it will be given to
> him. But when he asks, he must believe and not doubt, because
> he who doubts is like a wave of the sea, blown and tossed by
> the wind. That man should not think he will receive anything
> from the Lord; he is a double-minded man, unstable in all he
> does.   (James 1:5–8)*

To doubt is to make a big fuss before God about what you
want Him to do, and then, when the prayer is over, not believing a
word you said. It is being in a prayer meeting and saying, "God, I
believe You," and then leaving the meeting muttering, "I'm not sure
about what we prayed in there." You show that you don't believe
when you don't expect an answer or make arrangements for it.

The Scriptures tell us that we must believe. *"Let him ask of
God, who gives to all liberally and without reproach, and it will be
given to him. But let him ask in faith, with no doubting"* (James 1:5–6
NKJV). Instead of doubting, let us trust the generosity and kindness of God, putting our faith in His character and Word.

The Bible also says that if your *motives are wrong*, your prayers
will be hindered. *"When you ask, you do not receive, because you ask*

with wrong motives ["*ask amiss*" NKJV], *that you may spend what you get on your pleasures*" (James 4:3). What are your motives for praying? Are you asking God for something just so you can promote your own ego or for other selfish purposes? Or are you asking God to fulfill His Word so that His kingdom can come on the earth?

God knows we have needs, and it's not wrong to request that He fulfill them based on His Word. Jesus said, "*Your Father knows what you need before you ask him*" (Matthew 6:8). Yet our main focus should be honoring God and promoting His purposes. When we have our priorities right, we can trust Him to meet our daily needs. As Jesus exhorted us,

> *Do not worry, saying, "What shall we eat?" or "What shall we drink?" or "What shall we wear?" For the pagans run after all these things, and your heavenly Father knows that you need them. But seek first his kingdom and his righteousness, and all these things will be given to you as well.* (verses 31–33)

Therefore, when you pray, check your reasons for praying. Ask God to forgive you for any wrong motives you may have and to enable you to develop the right motives through the work of the Holy Spirit in your life. "*For it is God who works in you to will and to act according to his good purpose*" (Philippians 2:13).

⌒

Thought: Instead of doubting, trust the generosity and kindness of God, putting your faith in His character and Word.

Reading: Proverbs 3:5–6

BITTERNESS AND UNFORGIVENESS

"Let all bitterness, wrath, anger, clamor, and evil speaking be put away from you, with all malice."

—Ephesians 4:31 (NKJV)

Bitterness is a dangerous thing, especially as a hindrance to prayer. It often indicates a hidden hatred. To be bitter means to hold something against someone and not release that person through forgiveness. You hurt yourself more than the person against whom you are bitter. When you hold on to bitterness, it goes to the very source of your life and dries it up. Not only will you be weakened spiritually, but you will also begin to wither mentally, socially, and physically. It is like a cancer.

How does bitterness affect your prayer life? Remember, the Bible says, *"If I regard iniquity in my heart, the Lord will not hear me"* (Psalm 66:18 KJV). Bitterness is iniquity. God abhors iniquity more than sin, if a distinction between the two is possible. Iniquity is a special kind of sin. The Hebrew word for iniquity is *avon*. It means perversity or moral evil. Any rebellion against God is considered sin. However, iniquity is a vicious kind of sin that God specifically says He hates. In Hebrews 1:9, we read, *"Thou hast loved righteousness, and hated iniquity"* (KJV). The Greek word for *"iniquity"* in this verse is *anomia*, which means lawlessness or an offense against the law.

Bitterness is an especially hideous sin that can become deeply rooted. *"See to it that no one comes short of the grace of God; that no root of bitterness springing up causes trouble, and by it many become defiled"* (Hebrews 12:15 NASB). To guard against this sin and keep our prayers from being hindered, we need to maintain transparent, pure hearts before God and man.

Like bitterness, *unforgiveness* will hinder your prayers by blocking your relationships with God and other people. Mark 11:25 says, *"And when you stand praying, if you hold anything against anyone, forgive him, so that your Father in heaven may forgive you your sins."*

Unforgiveness can be an underlying presence in our lives, even when we don't realize we're harboring it in our hearts. Have you forgiven whoever it is that makes you angry every time you think about him or her? How about a member of the church who hurt you or a friend who still owes you money? How about someone on the job who wronged you—someone you're still mad at after three weeks, six months, or even ten years? How about an ex-husband, ex-wife, or former boyfriend or girlfriend? These things can block your prayer life because you are nurturing an unforgiving spirit. The Bible says, *"'In your anger do not sin': Do not let the sun go down while you are still angry, and do not give the devil a foothold"* (Ephesians 4:26–27). Unforgiveness does not reflect the character of Christ, and it demonstrates ingratitude for the vast forgiveness God has extended to you. Jesus made this point very clear in the parable of the unforgiving servant in Matthew 18:23–35. You need to resolve issues of unforgiveness in your life if you want God to hear your prayers.

⌒

Thought: To guard against bitterness, maintain a transparent, pure heart before God and man.

Reading: Luke 23:33–34

BROKEN FAMILY RELATIONSHIPS
AND IDOLATRY

"If it is possible, as far as it depends on you, live at peace with everyone." —Romans 12:18

Broken relationships in the home—between a husband and wife, for example—will also hinder prayers. First Peter 3:7 says, *"Husbands, in the same way be considerate as you live with your wives, and treat them with respect as the weaker partner and as heirs with you of the gracious gift of life, so that nothing will hinder your prayers."* Peter was saying, "Husbands, dwell with your wives with understanding, and don't let there be any animosity between you, lest your prayers be hindered."

Although he was speaking specifically to husbands, the same principle may be applied to relationships among all family members, since the law of unforgiveness applies to everyone. As believers, we have the Spirit of God dwelling within us. Therefore, we are to demonstrate the nature of God to one another. Psalm 103:8–10 tells us, *"The Lord is compassionate and gracious, slow to anger, abounding in love. He will not always accuse, nor will he harbor his anger forever; he does not treat us as our sins deserve or repay us according to our iniquities."* If we do not demonstrate the love, compassion, forgiveness, and grace of God to others, we are misrepresenting Him. How can we ask Him to fulfill His purposes by answering our prayers when we are violating those very purposes by the way we treat others?

An additional hindrance to prayer is to serve *"idols"* in our lives. Ezekiel 14:3 says, *"Son of man, these men have set up idols in their hearts and put wicked stumbling blocks before their faces. Should*

I let them inquire of me at all?" In this sobering verse, God is saying, "I will not answer your prayers if you are seeking idols." He is not speaking of statues. He is referring to idols of the heart. We must be careful not to set up idols in our lives, however subtle they may be.

Your television or cell phone can be an idol. Your car or clothes can be an idol. If you are married, your wife and children can be idols. If you are unmarried, your boyfriend or girlfriend can be an idol. Your reputation can be an idol. An idol is anything we give higher priority than God.

The displacement of God from His rightful position in our lives can happen gradually without our realizing it. We need to examine our lives to see what is most important to us, what our priorities are, and how we are spending our time. God deserves our primary love, respect, and devotion. *"Love the LORD your God with all your heart and with all your soul and with all your strength"* (Deuteronomy 6:5).

⸝

Thought: To fail to demonstrate the love, compassion, forgiveness, and grace of God to others is to misrepresent Him.

Reading: 1 Peter 3:1–12

— DAY 65 —

AN UNGENEROUS HEART

"Let us throw off everything that hinders and the sin that so easily entangles."   —Hebrews 12:1

Today, we look at a final area that can hinder our prayers: having *an ungenerous heart*. Proverbs 21:13 says, *"If a man shuts his ears to the cry of the poor, he too will cry out and not be answered."* God is telling us that if we are stingy, it can prevent our prayers from being heard. How can we ask God to provide for our needs when we're not concerned about the needs of those who are less fortunate than we are? However, if we are compassionate and generous, if we are givers, we can be assured that our prayers will be answered. *"A generous man will prosper; he who refreshes others will himself be refreshed"* (Proverbs 11:25). *"A generous man will himself be blessed, for he shares his food with the poor"* (Proverbs 22:9).

In addition, when we are generous toward God, He promises to provide for us abundantly:

> *"Bring the whole tithe into the storehouse, that there may be food in my house. Test me in this," says the LORD Almighty, "and see if I will not throw open the floodgates of heaven and pour out so much blessing that you will not have room enough for it."* (Malachi 3:10)

Hebrews 12:1 says, *"Let us throw off* ["lay aside" KJV, NKJV] ***everything that hinders** and the sin that so easily entangles, and let us run with perseverance the race marked out for us."* Let us determine, through God's grace, to remove all hindrances from our lives so we can live in harmony with God and others, and have confidence and effectiveness in prayer.

Let's pray together:

Heavenly Father,

As Your Word says, we are burdened by things that hinder us spiritually and emotionally, and we too easily become entangled with sin. These encumbrances keep us from having a joyful, unbroken relationship with You and with our family members, friends, coworkers, and others. We ask You to enable us to have a true understanding of who we are in Your Son, Jesus Christ. Help us to clear away each of the hindrances in our lives so we can live freely as Your children and so we can pray in harmony with Your will and purposes for the world. We ask this in the name of Jesus, who is our Burden-Bearer—who has carried our sins and sorrows, who has healed us by His own wounds, and whose suffering on our behalf has brought us peace with You, according to Isaiah 53:4–5. Amen.

Thought: How can we ask God to provide for our needs when we're not concerned about the needs of those who are less fortunate than we are?

Reading: Malachi 3:7–11

— Day 66 —

THE POWER OF THE WORD

"For the word of the cross is foolishness to those who are perishing, but to us who are being saved it is the power of God." —1 Corinthians 1:18 (NASB)

We must never forget the true power sources behind prayer: God's Word, the name of Jesus, and the indwelling Holy Spirit. For the rest of this devotional, we will look at these power sources in more depth.

God wants to use His power in the world. However, for Him to do so through us, we must first understand how to appropriate His Word. We have learned that the heart of prayer is asking God to intervene in the world to fulfill His eternal purposes for mankind. Interwoven throughout this devotional has been the principle that we are to pray to God *on the basis of His Word*—the revelation of who He is, what His will is, and what He has promised.

As we have seen, the key to effective prayer is understanding God's purpose for your life—as a human being in general, and as an individual specifically. In this way, God's will can become the authority of your prayers. True prayer is calling forth what God has already purposed and predestined—the establishment of His plans for the earth. That means that whatever we ask God to do in our lives, in the lives of others, or in the world must be based on His will. God's purpose is to be both the motivation and the content of our prayers. Thus, *God's purpose is the "raw material" of prayer.*

It is through God's Word that we can know, believe, and agree in faith with God's will. Without His Word, our prayers have no foundation. They are based merely on our opinions, desires, and feelings rather than on *"the living and enduring word of God"* (1 Peter 1:23). Such prayers are powerless to effect change. However, all the power of God is at the disposal of true prayer.

Prayer is actually very simple. It is speaking God's Word to Him exactly as He gave it to us. There is no difference between what the people in the Bible were given by God as the basis for their effective prayers and what you and I are given to work with. They relied on what God has given all mankind—His Word.

Since God has already given us His Word, our job is to learn how to handle it properly and responsibly. (See 2 Timothy 2:15.) Because we receive the same raw material for prayer that other believers have received, our effectiveness or ineffectiveness in prayer often has to do with how we handle God's Word. It is how we use what God has given us that can make the difference between answered and unanswered prayer. We can use God's Word correctly only when we understand what it is and how to apply it. We will explore these themes over the next several days.

⌒

Thought: Prayer is actually very simple. It is speaking God's Word to Him exactly as He gave it to us.

Reading: 2 Timothy 3:16–17

GOD SPEAKS THROUGH THE WORD

*"When you received the word of God,...you accepted it not as
the word of men, but as it actually is, the word of God."*
—1 Thessalonians 2:13

To understand the power of God's Word in prayer, we must
first recognize that *God Himself is speaking in the Word,* because
the Word is who He is: *"In the beginning was the Word, and the
Word was with God, and the Word was God"* (John 1:1). Therefore,
God's presence becomes a part of our prayers when we speak His
Word in faith.

In 1 Kings 19, we read that Elijah did not find God in the
wind, earthquake, or fire but in *"a still small voice"* (verse 12 KJV,
NKJV). While many people want to see a manifestation of God's
power, they fail to realize that His Word is the foundation of that
power—*that the power is only a reflection of the greatness of God
Himself.* It was His *"still small voice"* that was behind the forces of
nature that Elijah saw. The power of God's Word is so great that
if our faith is the size of a mustard seed, mountains can be moved.
(See Matthew 17:20.)

Second, *the Word reveals God's nature*—and it is His nature
that reflects His will. Everything God says is a revelation of His
character and purposes. Again, He and His Word cannot be separated. That is why God's fulfillment of His Word is a matter of
personal integrity for Him.

The question for us is this: how will we respond to what the
Word reveals about God's character? Numbers 23:19 says, *"God is
not a man, that he should lie, nor a son of man, that he should change
his mind. Does he speak and then not act? Does he promise and not*

fulfill?" Do we believe that God is honorable and that He will keep His Word? A cardinal principle of answered prayer is belief in the trustworthiness of the One to whom you're praying. The power of your prayers depends on it. The Word will work in your life only as you believe it:

> And we also thank God continually because, when you received the word of God, which you heard from us, you accepted it not as the word of men, but as it actually is, the word of God, **which is at work in you who believe.**
>
> (1 Thessalonians 2:13)

What do you demonstrate about your belief (or disbelief) in God? If God promises something, but you don't believe it will come to pass, you're telling Him, "I have no confidence in You." You may think, "Oh, I would never say that to God!" Yet you might actually be saying that to Him all the time by not believing His Word.

Your belief is evidence that you trust God. He is not impressed by how many Scriptures you quote or how long you pray. He is moved and convinced when you believe what He has told you, and when you prove it by acting on it. *Belief is trust in action.*

⌒

Thought: A cardinal principle of answered prayer is belief in the trustworthiness of the One to whom you're praying.

Reading: John 1:1–4

THE WORD IS ALIVE

"The word of God is living and active. Sharper than any double-edged sword...."   —Hebrews 4:12

There is power in the Word because it is not just knowledge and facts to us; it is life itself:

> *Take to heart all the words I have solemnly declared to you this day, so that you may command your children to obey carefully all the words of this law. They are not just idle words for you—they are your life.*   (Deuteronomy 32:46–47)

> *The Spirit gives life; the flesh counts for nothing. The words I have spoken to you are spirit and they are life.*   (John 6:63)

> *The word of God is living and active. Sharper than any double-edged sword, it penetrates even to dividing soul and spirit, joints and marrow; it judges the thoughts and attitudes of the heart.*   (Hebrews 4:12)

The Word is alive—that's how powerful it is! What did God use to create the world? "[The Word] *was with God in the beginning. Through him all things were made; without him nothing was made that has been made*" (John 1:2–3).

What did God give Moses that made him so successful? "*When the* LORD *saw that he had gone over to look,* **God called to him** *from within the bush, 'Moses! Moses!' And Moses said, 'Here I am'*" (Exodus 3:4; see also verses 5–10).

What did God give Ezekiel to make him a powerful prophet? Fifty times in the book of Ezekiel, the prophet reported, "*The word of the* LORD *came to me.*" (See, for example, Ezekiel 3:16; 6:1; 12:1.)

What did God send to the world to redeem it? *"The Word became flesh and made his dwelling among us. We have seen his glory, the glory of the One and Only, who came from the Father, full of grace and truth"* (John 1:14).

What did Jesus give His disciples for salvation and sanctification? *"Whoever hears my word and believes him who sent me has eternal life and will not be condemned; he has crossed over from death to life"* (John 5:24). *"You are already clean because of the word I have spoken to you"* (John 15:3). *"Sanctify them by the truth; your word is truth"* (John 17:17).

What did the disciples use to continue Jesus's ministry on earth?

> *"Now, Lord, consider their threats and **enable your servants to speak your word** with great boldness." …After they prayed, the place where they were meeting was shaken. And they were all filled with the Holy Spirit and **spoke the word of God boldly**.* (Acts 4:29, 31)

The Word is alive and active on our behalf. Probably no one quoted Scripture more than Jesus did. When He was tempted by the devil in the wilderness, what did He do? Each time, He gave the devil God's Word, saying, *"It is written."* (See Matthew 4:4, 7, 10.) Jesus was so well acquainted with the Word that He wasn't fooled by the enemy's distortion of it. (See verse 6.) God watches over His Word to fulfill it. (See Jeremiah 1:12.) That is why, when Jesus spoke the Word in faith, God fulfilled it, and Christ overcame temptation.

⌒

Thought: The Word is alive—that's how powerful it is!

Reading: Matthew 4:1–11

— Day 69 —

ABIDING IN THE WORD

"I am the vine, you are the branches. He who abides in Me, and I in him, bears much fruit; for without Me you can do nothing."   —John 15:5 (NKJV)

If you truly want the Word to work powerfully in your life, you have to make sure it is inside you. Jesus said, *"If you abide in Me, and My words abide* [are living] *in you, you will ask what you desire, and it shall be done for you"* (John 15:7 NKJV). Perhaps you've read this verse and tried it, but it didn't work. Maybe you don't even bother trying to apply this verse to your life anymore; it's just a nice-sounding Scripture to you. Yet Christ was giving us the key to success. What's the first word in the verse? *"If."* We like the *"it shall be done"* part, but we often forget the *"if."*

There are two conditions to answered prayer: *"If you abide in Me,"* and *"If…My words abide in you."* First, what does it mean for you to abide in Jesus? It means to constantly flow in spiritual communion with Him. You do this by fellowshipping with Him and worshipping Him, by praying and fasting.

Second, what does it mean to have His words abiding or living in you? Here is how you can test whether or not the Word is in you: what is the first thing that comes out of your mouth when you are under pressure? Is it an affirmation of faith? Or is it fear, confusion, frustration, doubt, or anger? We know the Word is truly inside us when it directs our thoughts and actions.

You can't get the Word inside you by keeping it on a shelf in your house. You can't get the Word in your spirit by putting it under your pillow at night and expecting to absorb it by osmosis. You can't even get the Word in you by having someone preach it to you. Preaching only stirs up faith. You need to have the Word in you already. You need to be reading and meditating on the Word regularly.

Jesus gave us the condition *"If...My words abide in you,"* so that the last part of the verse having to do with prayer could be fulfilled in us: *"ask what you desire, and it shall be done for you."* If His words are in you, then what you desire and ask for will reflect those words. Do you remember the connection? If you are filled with the Word, then you won't ask for just anything you feel like. You will ask on the basis of His Word, which is what He watches over to fulfill.

God fulfills His Word, and nothing else. He doesn't fulfill your suggestions or feelings. Therefore, if you don't bring Him His Word, you won't be able to experience *"it shall be done for you."* Too often, we think the phrase *"ask what you desire"* means we can ask for anything. Yet Christ was saying, in effect, "If My Word is abiding in you, then you can ask for what's abiding in you, and it will be done." That is the power of the Word.

⌣

Thought: If Jesus's words are in you, then what you desire and ask for will reflect those words.

Reading: John 15:5–8

THE WORD BUILDS FAITH

"Man does not live on bread alone, but on every word that comes from the mouth of God." —Matthew 4:4

Go d's Word is our source of prayer power because it produces in us what pleases God and causes Him to respond to our requests: *faith.* As we have already seen, God's Word is the parent of all faith. *"Faith comes from hearing the message, and the message is heard through the word of Christ"* (Romans 10:17). *"By faith we understand that the universe was formed at God's command, so that what is seen was not made out of what was visible"* (Hebrews 11:3). Faith is the result of dwelling in and on the Word of God. When the Word of God is lived and practiced in our lives, it becomes power to us.

For the rest of your life, your goal should be to build your faith because the Bible makes it clear that faith is how we live: *"The righteous will live by his faith"* (Habakkuk 2:4; see also Romans 1:17; Galatians 3:11; Hebrews 10:38). We live by faith, not by sight. (See 2 Corinthians 5:7.)

I have been crucified with Christ and I no longer live, but Christ lives in me. The life I live in the body, I live by faith in the Son of God, who loved me and gave himself for me.

(Galatians 2:20)

You have to work on this thing called faith—faith in God and in His Word. Jesus said, *"It is written: 'Man does not live on bread alone, but on every word that comes from the mouth of God'"* (Matthew 4:4). Your faith needs to be fed. It needs to feed on the Word if you are to be spiritually sustained. Feed your faith by filling it with God's Word, and then make sure you act on that Word. This is very important. The word of man is what man is; the Word of God is what God is. If you want to live like a child of God, then you have to believe His Word.

Having faith means having total conviction concerning God's promises to man. Believing God is simply taking God at His Word, making requests based on His Word, and then acting as if you own the title deed to what He has promised. Remember that it is better, safer, healthier, and more reasonable to live by faith than to live by doubt or wishful thinking. People who live by doubt and wishful thinking experience high blood pressure, frustration, tension, and anger. They are angry at the world because they can't see anything beyond their weak hope. However, when you live by faith, you will defy the world's understanding. You will have peace and joy even when you experience difficult situations. Like Jesus during the tempest at sea, you will be able to sleep in the middle of a storm! (See Mark 4:35–41.)

Thought: God's Word is the foundation of His power. His power is a reflection of His greatness.

Reading: Hebrews 11:8–12

— DAY 71 —

GOD WORKS FOR YOUR GOOD

"If God is for us, who can be against us?"   —Romans 8:31

I never use the word *problems* anymore. Why? It is because I understand that everything in the world is under God's command, including the devil. That is why the Bible says, *"We know that in all things God works for the good of those who love him, who have been called according to his purpose"* (Romans 8:28). Everything works for my good, no matter what it is, because I'm called according to God's purpose and will.

It is God's will that I live confidently in the knowledge that God *"calls things that are not as though they were"* (Romans 4:17). If I live only by what I see, I am living in sin. *"Everything that does not come from faith is sin"* (Romans 14:23). There are many such sinners in the church—people who are in rebellion against God's will because they are living only by what they see. Faith grows out of one thing—the Word of God.

God has promised certain things, and all His promises are already "yes." (See 2 Corinthians 1:18–20.) In other words, He wants to give you everything He promised. Some of the promises in the Bible were spoken to a specific person or group of people. Yet the Bible indicates that Jesus made His promises accessible to everybody. *"No matter how many promises God has made, they are 'Yes' in Christ"* (2 Corinthians 1:20). Jesus made the contract, which God gave to a specific person or group, everyone's contract. However, you have to qualify in the same way they had to qualify—by using your faith. Once you know the promise, you don't have to say, "If it is God's will." That is why praying the Word is so important.

If you have faith in God's Word, God will take what is "impossible" and make it seem like an everyday thing. Your "problem" circumstance excites God because He knows you now have to rely on faith, which will enable you to receive His promise. God's dreams are always in contrast to your difficulties. God knows what things look like to you. He gives you the promise ahead of the blessing so that when it comes, you'll know it came from Him.

Everything I have, I have received through prayer. When you pray God's Word in faith, things that have been bound up will suddenly open up. You will say, "But I had been trying to accomplish that for ten years!" Yes, but you hadn't prayed according to God's Word and trusted in God's faithfulness until now. Belief will open doors that even hard work cannot unlock. God says if you believe Him, He is going to give you the best of the land. (See Genesis 45:18.)

⌒

Thought: When you pray God's Word in faith, things that have been bound up will suddenly open up.

Reading: 1 Peter 5:6–7

SPEAKING GOD'S WORDS

"I write these things to you who believe in the name of the Son of God so that you may know that you have eternal life."
—1 John 5:13

Let's look at what could be considered the ultimate passage on prayer. First John 5:13–15 pulls together everything we have been discussing in this devotional. It begins, *"I write these things to you who believe in the name of the Son of God…"* (verse 13). Does this verse apply to you? If you believe in the name of the Son of God, it does. The passage continues, *"…so that you may know that you have eternal life"* (verse 13). John was saying, "I'm writing these things so that you can know you are connected to God." Then he said, *"This is the confidence we have in approaching God…"* (verse 14). What is that confidence? *"That if we ask anything according to his will, he hears us"* (verse 14).

Here's that conditional word *"if"* again: *"If we ask anything according to his will…."* God's Word is His will. His Word is His desire, His desire is His intent, and His intent is His purpose. *"If we ask anything according to his will, he hears us."* You can be sure God always hears your prayers—100 percent of the time—when you pray according to His will. Who does God hear when you pray His Word? He hears Himself. God will hear you when He hears the words He Himself has spoken.

Is there anything more important in prayer than for God to hear you? The passage tells us what happens when this takes place: *"And if we know that he hears us—whatever we ask—we know that **we have** what we asked of him"* (1 John 5:15).

God's plan for your life is even bigger than your plan. However, to enter into that plan, you have to believe in it and affirm it by what you say. The reason Jesus's life was so successful was that He didn't speak His own words—He spoke God's words.

For I did not speak of my own accord, but the Father who sent me commanded me what to say and how to say it. I know that his command leads to eternal life. So whatever I say is just what the Father has told me to say. (John 12:49–50)

The words I say to you are not just my own. Rather, it is the Father, living in me, who is doing his work. (John 14:10)

Do we need anything clearer than this? This is the secret to living a victorious life of faith. It was a major key to Jesus's power on earth. Jesus Christ didn't invent words to say. He was always praying to God what God had said first. Why? Again, it is because God watches over His Word to fulfill it. Jesus's works were the Father's works because His words were the Father's words. His miracles were the Father's miracles because His words were the Father's words. He knew who He was, what He believed, and what to say, and that combination brought Him victory on earth.

The same can be true for us if we follow His example.

⌒

Thought: Speaking the Father's words was the primary secret to Jesus's power.

Reading: John 12:44–50

THE WORD TESTIFIES TO PRAYER

"For everything that was written in the past was written to teach us, so that through endurance and the encouragement of the Scriptures we might have hope." —Romans 15:4

The Bible builds faith—and therefore gives power—because it is the greatest Book ever written testifying to how God answers the faith-filled prayers of His people. Hebrews 11:1–2 says that *"the ancients"* were commended for the fact that they did not live by what they could see but by what God had told them. They believed it and acted upon it, and it worked.

The men and women of the Bible were not super-saints. They were people just like us. They received answers to prayer as they put their faith in God, trusting in His character and Word. The Bible makes this very clear:

Elijah was a man just like us. He prayed earnestly that it would not rain, and it did not rain on the land for three and a half years. Again he prayed, and the heavens gave rain, and the earth produced its crops. (James 5:17–18)

It is through the powerful examples of believers in the Bible that we are encouraged to have faith that God can and will intervene on our behalf. Here are just a few examples:

A servant (Abraham's chief servant) and a king (Solomon) both asked for wisdom, and God gave it in each case. (See Genesis 24:1–27; 1 Kings 3:4–14.)

Hannah asked God for blessing and deliverance from her distress, and God granted her request. (See 1 Samuel 1:1–20.)

Moses and Daniel interceded for the nation of Israel, and God heard and answered in His mercy. (See Exodus 32:1–14; Daniel 9.)

Nehemiah prayed for the restoration of Jerusalem and was granted favor and protection in his work to rebuild the walls. (See the book of Nehemiah.)

Paul and Cornelius received knowledge concerning the way of salvation after they had prayed. (See Acts 9:1–20, especially verse 11; Acts 10.)

Jesus at His baptism (see Luke 3:21–22) and the disciples at Pentecost (see Acts 1:14; 2:1–4) received the Holy Spirit after prayer.

Peter and John both received revelation and insight while they were praying. (See Acts 10:9–15; 11:1–18; Revelation 1:9–11.)

Paul and Silas were delivered from prison after praying and singing to God. (See Acts 16:16–34.)

We know from reading about the lives of these believers that many of them struggled with doubts, were inclined to mistakes and failures, and had to learn by experience. However, we also see the faithfulness and love of God in teaching them His ways, coming to their aid, and strengthening them for the purposes He had in mind for them. The Bible is filled with stories of the power of God to save, heal, and bless. These accounts are God's faith messages to us, telling us that He will intervene on our behalf, also. We are His beloved children; we have been redeemed by His Son and are being prepared to rule and reign with Him in eternity.

Thought: The men and women of the Bible received answers to prayer as they put their faith in God, trusting in His character and Word.

Reading: James 5:13–18

THE WORD PREPARES US FOR PRAYER

"I rejoice at Your word as one who finds great treasure."
—Psalm 119:162 (NKJV)

God's Word gives power by enabling us to prepare for prayer and to maintain communion with God. Psalm 119 tells us that when we wholeheartedly embrace the Word, it will keep our lives in line with God's will so that nothing will hinder us from walking in His ways and receiving answers to our prayers: *"Blessed are they who keep his statutes and seek him with all their heart. They do nothing wrong; they walk in his ways.... I have hidden your word in my heart that I might not sin against you"* (verses 2–3, 11).

We need to offer our lives as living sacrifices to God every day so we can have continual fellowship with Him. *"Offer your bodies as living sacrifices, holy and pleasing to God—this is your spiritual act of worship"* (Romans 12:1). Then, as our minds are transformed by reading and meditating on the Word, we will know the will of God, and we will pray confidently and effectively:

> *Do not conform any longer to the pattern of this world, but be transformed by the renewing of your mind.* **Then you will be able to test and approve what God's will is—his good, pleasing and perfect will.** (Romans 12:2)

What a tremendous gift the Word of God is to us! It gives us the power to know and do the will of God, the power to pray with certainty and boldness in all situations, and the power to know that God hears us when we pray according to His will. *"And if we know that he hears us—whatever we ask—we know that we have what we asked of him"* (1 John 5:15).

Let's pray together:

Heavenly Father,

In Matthew 13:23, Jesus said that those who hear the Word and receive it, those who allow it to sink into their hearts, are like good soil. Yet the power is in the Word. It is the Word that will bring forth good fruit in us and spring up within us to everlasting life. We ask You to fulfill Your Word in our lives. Make us good soil that brings forth good fruit. Your Word has caused us to believe that You answer prayer offered in faith and according to Your will. We set ourselves in agreement with You that everything we pray for will be answered "yes." We will both expect and prepare for the answer. Give us the confidence that if You said it, You will do it; if You promised it, it will come to pass. Thank You for Your Word. Thank You for the faith that You have given us. Help us to expect a miracle. We pray this in the name of Jesus, our High Priest, who sits at Your right hand and intercedes for us. Amen.

Thought: What a tremendous gift the Word of God is to us!

Reading: Psalm 119:1–16

— DAY 75 —
THE POWER OF JESUS'S NAME

"Salvation is found in no one else, for there is no other name under heaven given to mankind by which we must be saved."
—Acts 4:12 (NIV2011)

There is no other name under heaven given to mankind...." One of the most important elements of effective prayer is using the name of Jesus. In conjunction with praying according to the Word, praying in the name of Jesus gives our prayers tremendous power. Yet we must be able to legally use the authority behind Jesus's name in order to obtain results in prayer.

Many believers aren't receiving answers to their prayers because they misunderstand what it means to pray in the name of Jesus. We tend to think we can pray any type of prayer and then say, "In the name of Jesus, amen," believing that the phrase alone is what makes our prayers effective with God. It doesn't work that way. We shouldn't try to dignify or sanctify our prayers by merely tacking on the name of Jesus at the end. Remember, Jesus's name is not a magic formula or password that guarantees automatic acceptance of all our prayers. When the Bible says we are to pray in the name of Jesus, it's not referring to the word *J-e-s-u-s*, as such, because that's just the English word for the name of the Son of God; other languages translate His name using different words. It's not the word but what the name represents that makes the difference.

Therefore, we're not effective in prayer just by using the word *Jesus* but in understanding the significance of who He really is and appropriating His power through faith in His name. We see a clear demonstration of this truth in the account of the sons of Sceva in the book of Acts:

> Some Jews who went around driving out evil spirits tried to invoke the name of the Lord Jesus over those who were demon-possessed. They would say, "In the name of Jesus, whom Paul preaches, I command you to come out." Seven sons of Sceva, a Jewish chief priest, were doing this. One day the evil spirit answered them, "Jesus I know, and I know about Paul, but who are you?" Then the man who had the evil spirit jumped on them and overpowered them all. He gave them such a beating that they ran out of the house naked and bleeding. When this became known to the Jews and Greeks living in Ephesus, they were all seized with fear, and the name of the Lord Jesus was held in high honor.   (Acts 19:13–17)

This story reveals that someone can use the name *Jesus* all they want, but they will still have no authority over the devil if (1) they aren't in proper relationship with Christ, and (2) they don't understand how to use Jesus's name. Are you praying based on the righteousness of Christ or on your own merits? Do you understand who Jesus is, and do you believe in His authority and power? It doesn't work to pray in Jesus's name without knowing who He is and praying in faith according to that knowledge.

⌣

Thought: We must be able to legally use the authority behind the power of Jesus's name in order to obtain results in prayer.

Reading: Luke 10:1–20

OUR COVENANTAL RIGHTS

"But as many as received him, to them gave he power to become the sons of God, even to them that believe on his name."
—John 1:12 (KJV)

God does not owe us anything. We have no claim on Him outside Christ's work of grace on our behalf. Christ redeemed us from our sins, or trespasses. (See Ephesians 1:7.) When you trespass, you are doing something illegal. Similarly, someone who doesn't know God or is not in proper relationship with God through Christ cannot legally do business with God. Yet because of Jesus, we can be forgiven of our trespasses. He canceled our sins through His sacrifice on the cross and delivered us from the power of sin, so now we can have legal access to God through His name. No one can claim power through Jesus's name without having official child-of-God status. *"But as many as received him, to them gave he power to become the sons of God, even to them that believe on his name"* (John 1:12 KJV).

The authority we have in Jesus's name through prayer is a covenantal authority; it is based on our covenant relationship with God through Christ. *"But the ministry Jesus has received is as superior to theirs [the priests of Israel] as the covenant of which he is mediator is superior to the old one, and it is founded on better promises"* (Hebrews 8:6). We can pray to God directly in Jesus's name because He has given us authority to do so based on the new covenant. Seven times in the New Testament, Jesus made a statement such as the following, giving us the legal right to use His name with God:

> *In that day you will no longer ask me anything. I tell you the truth, my Father will give you whatever you ask in my name.*

Until now you have not asked for anything in my name. Ask and you will receive, and your joy will be complete. Though I have been speaking figuratively, a time is coming when I will no longer use this kind of language but will tell you plainly about my Father. In that day you will ask in my name. I am not saying that I will ask the Father on your behalf. No, the Father himself loves you because you have loved me and have believed that I came from God. (John 16:23–27)

Therefore, the strength of prayers prayed in the name of Jesus is covenantal authority. We pray to the Father based on our relationship with Christ, who is Lord over the new covenant. Philippians 2:10 says, *"That at the name of Jesus every knee should bow, in heaven and on earth and under the earth."* Because Christ restored us to our relationship and rights with both God and the earth, His name is our legal authority—whether we are dealing with *"heaven"* (with God), *"earth"* (with men), or he who is *"under the earth"* (with Satan).

In essence, Jesus's name is our legal authority to transact spiritual business with God. *"For there is one God and one mediator between God and men, the man Christ Jesus, who gave himself as a ransom for all men—the testimony given in its proper time"* (1 Timothy 2:5–6).

⌒

Thought: The authority we have in Jesus's name is a covenantal authority based on our covenant relationship with God through Christ.

Reading: John 3:16–18

WHAT'S IN A NAME?

"No one is like you, O Lord; you are great, and your name is mighty in power." —Jeremiah 10:6

To understand the power of Jesus's name, we need to be aware of the Bible's emphasis on the meaning of names. In the Scriptures, the name of someone usually symbolized the essence of their nature. It represented the person's collective attributes and characteristics—their nature, power, and glory.

For example, God gave Adam the privilege of naming Eve—of encapsulating Eve's attributes. Adam actually named Eve twice—the first time as a description of her origin and the second time as a description of who she would become in fulfillment of her purpose. First, he said, *"This is now bone of my bones and flesh of my flesh; she shall be called 'woman,' for she was taken out of man"* (Genesis 2:23). Later, the Bible says, *"Adam named his wife Eve, because she would become the mother of all the living"* (Genesis 3:20). The Hebrew word for Eve is *chavvah,* meaning "life-giver." Her name describes the essence of her nature as the mother of mankind.

At times, God would *change* the names of His people to reflect the promises He had made to them and the purposes He had for them, which went far beyond their own or their parents' expectations.

+ In Genesis 17:4–5, Abram's name, which means "exalted father" or "high father," was changed to Abraham, meaning "father of a multitude," reflecting the promise that *"Abraham will surely become a great and powerful nation, and all nations on earth will be blessed through him"* (Genesis 18:18).

- In Genesis 32:27–28, Jacob's name, which means "supplanter," was changed to Israel, meaning "he will rule as God" or "a prince of God." This reflected the fact that the great nation of Israel would come from his line—the nation that was meant to be God's earthly representative by being *"a kingdom of priests and a holy nation"* (Exodus 19:6).

- In John 1:42, Jesus changed Simon's name, which is derived from a Hebrew word meaning "hearing," to Cephas, meaning "a rock" or "a stone." The English translation of this word is "Peter." Peter's new name signified his role in establishing and leading the church in its infancy. (See Matthew 16:18.)

Why does God put such emphasis on people's names? It is because mankind is made in His image, and He places great significance on His own name. Using our earlier definition, God's name symbolizes the essence of His nature. It represents His collective attributes and characteristics—His nature, power, and glory. The main reason we are commanded not to use the name of God in vain (see Exodus 20:7) is that His name does not just *represent* who He is but, also, it *is* who He is.

Thought: In the Bible, a person's name symbolized the essence of their nature.

Reading: Malachi 1:11

"I AM HAS SENT ME"

*"God said to Moses, 'I AM WHO I AM. This is what you are
to say to the Israelites: "I AM has sent me to you."'"*
—Exodus 3:14

God revealed tremendous truths about His name to Moses:

*Moses said to God, "Suppose I go to the Israelites and say to
them, 'The God of your fathers has sent me to you,' and they
ask me, 'What is his name?' Then what shall I tell them?"
God said to Moses, "I AM WHO I AM. This is what you are
to say to the Israelites: 'I AM has sent me to you.'" God also
said to Moses, "Say to the Israelites, 'The LORD, the God of
your fathers—the God of Abraham, the God of Isaac and the
God of Jacob—has sent me to you.' This is my name forever,
the name by which I am to be remembered from generation to
generation."*   (Exodus 3:13–15)

The Lord was saying, "I *am* My name. Whatever I am, that's
what I'm called." When you translate this concept into English, it
goes something like this: "My name is whatever I am at the time
I am it." This is because God is our all-sufficiency, and His name
differs depending on what our need is at a particular time. That is
the reason there are so many names attributed to God in the Old
Testament. Yet God's overarching name, I AM, encompasses all
His nature and attributes.

In effect, God is telling us, "If you need bread, then pray,
'Father, You are my Bread.' When you acknowledge that I am your
Provider and Sustenance, then I become Bread to you. If you are

thirsty, then pray, 'Father, You are my Water.' I manifest the characteristic of whatever you need."

Moreover, by calling Himself *"the God of Abraham, the God of Isaac and the God of Jacob"* (Exodus 3:15), the Lord affirms that He is a personal God who meets individual human needs. He is the God of real people—Abraham, Isaac, and Jacob. In the same way, He desires to be your God and to meet your individual needs, no matter what they are.

Living by faith sometimes means declaring what seems to us like the strangest things. For example, the Bible says, *"Let the weak say, 'I am strong'"* (Joel 3:10 NKJV). We're weak, but God tells us to proclaim the opposite. He says, "Call on My strength. Call Me Jehovah Omnipotent." He isn't telling us to just use His name; He's calling on us to understand His nature and to appropriate it by faith. It is not God's nature to be weak. If you are experiencing weakness, then you must call on the Lord your Strength. (See Psalm 18:1.) If you are experiencing poverty, you must call on Jehovah-Jireh, your Provider. (See Genesis 22:8.) If your body is sick, you need to call on Jehovah-Rapha, the God who heals. (See Exodus 15:26.) God is telling us not to dwell on the problem but on His attribute that addresses the problem. Since He is the I Am, His attributes are as numerous as your needs—and beyond!

~

Thought: God says, in essence, "I *am* My name. Whatever I am, that's what I'm called."

Reading: Micah 4:5

THE NAMES OF JESUS

"'I tell you the truth,' Jesus answered, 'before Abraham was born, I am!'" —John 8:58

How does the Bible's emphasis on the meanings of names—especially God's name—apply to praying in the name of Jesus? Since a person's name represents their collective attributes and characteristics, the names of the second person of the Trinity refer to all that He is, both as the Son of God and as the Son of Man—all of His nature, power, and glory.

Jesus Christ is the revelation of God in human form. Because He is fully divine as well as fully human, He is ascribed a variety of names, just as His Father is. For example, in the Old Testament, some of His names are the *"Seed"* (Genesis 3:15 NKJV), *"the BRANCH"* (Zechariah 6:12), and *"Immanuel* ["God with us"]" (Isaiah 7:14). In the New Testament, the Son has many designations, but the first we read about is the name *Jesus*.

The name *Jesus* means "Savior." Jesus was called Savior because He came to earth as a human being to accomplish the salvation of the world. *"He will save his people from their sins"* (Matthew 1:21). Therefore, *Jesus* is the name of Christ in His humanity—as the Son of Man. However, *I AM* is the name of Christ in His divinity—as the Son of God. *"'I tell you the truth,' Jesus answered, 'before Abraham was born, I am!'"* (John 8:58).

On one occasion, Jesus said, *"I am the bread of life"* (John 6:35). Not long afterward, He indicated that He is also the water of life: *"If anyone is thirsty, let him come to me and drink"* (John 7:37). He referred to Himself as *"the way and the truth and the life"* (John 14:6) because He enables us to have access to the Father and receive spiritual life. He called Himself *"the true vine"* (John 15:1) because only by remaining in Him can we bear spiritual fruit. As with God the Father, the attributes that Jesus manifests reveal His glory and correspond to His people's needs.

What prompted Jesus to say to Martha, *"I am the resurrection and the life. He who believes in me will live even though he dies; and whoever lives and believes in me will never die"* (John 11:25–26)? It was because He was confronted with the reality of the death of her brother, Lazarus. Jesus's name addressed the need at hand, and He raised Lazarus from the dead.

Here is the key: *If we want God to meet our need when we pray "in the name of Jesus," we must pray based on the divine name that meets our particular need at the time.* This is how our prayers are answered. We don't receive answers to prayer by merely speaking Jesus's name but by calling on His nature and attributes, which can meet our every need.

⌒

Thought: If we want God to meet our need when we pray "in the name of Jesus," we must pray based on the divine name that meets our particular need.

Reading: John 11:1–45

POWER OF ATTORNEY

"I tell you the truth, my Father will give you whatever you ask in my name." —John 16:23

Legally, when you grant power of attorney to someone, it means that you appoint that person to represent you. You give the person the legal right and authority to speak for you and to do business in your name. Praying in the name of Jesus is giving Him "power of attorney" to intercede on your behalf when you make requests of the Father. Jesus said,

> I tell you the truth, my Father will give you whatever you ask in my name. Until now you have not asked for anything in my name. Ask and you will receive, and your joy will be complete. (John 16:23–24)

When Christ Jesus was on earth, His disciples didn't need to pray to the Father. When they required food, Jesus provided it. When Peter's mother-in-law was sick, Jesus healed her. When they needed to pay taxes, Jesus supplied the money. When they needed a place to meet, Jesus had already made preparations for it. When they were with Jesus, they had everything they needed. If they wanted something, they asked Him for it directly. However, Jesus was returning to the Father, and they would no longer be able to ask Him for anything directly. They would need to pray to the Father, and Jesus instructed them to do so in His name. Why? It is because the Father works through Christ.

Jesus is now actively working on our behalf from His position at the right hand of the Father. (See, for example, Romans 8:34.) He is representing our interests to God: *"Therefore he is able to save* completely those who come to God through him, because he always lives to intercede for them" (Hebrews 7:25). He is bringing glory to the Father by fulfilling the prayers we pray according to the Word.

In addition to speaking to His disciples about praying in His name, Jesus talked to them about the Holy Spirit because the Spirit continues Jesus's ministry on earth. *"If you love me, you will obey what I command. And I will ask the Father, and he will give you another Counselor* ["Comforter" KJV] *to be with you forever—the Spirit of truth"* (John 14:15–17). Jesus was saying, in effect, "I am going to the Father, but I will send you the Holy Spirit. He will be your Counselor. He will assist in exercising power of attorney by enabling you to pray. He will help you present your cases to the Father in My name."

Throughout the New Testament, we find references to the work of the Holy Spirit. One of the repeated themes is that when we do not know what we should pray for, the Holy Spirit helps us in our weakness:

> *We do not know what we ought to pray for, but the Spirit himself intercedes for us with groans that words cannot express. And he who searches our hearts knows the mind of the Spirit, because the Spirit intercedes for the saints in accordance with God's will.* (Romans 8:26–27)

As you pray in the name of Jesus, think of Jesus as your Power of Attorney, and rely on the intercession of the Holy Spirit in making your requests.

Thought: The Holy Spirit continues Jesus's ministry on earth, including assisting us in prayer when we don't know how to pray.

Reading: Jude 1:20–21

JESUS'S NAME IS THE KEY TO HEAVEN

"Therefore God exalted [Jesus] to the highest place and gave him the name that is above every name." —Philippians 2:9

One of the things Jesus emphasized is that *"the Father loves the Son"* (John 3:35; 5:20). This is a crucial truth in prayer because, if the Father loves the Son, then the Father will do anything the Son wants. If the Father loves the Son and does whatever the Son asks, and if the Son is representing you, then you don't have to worry about your case being heard. That is why it is essential that you call upon Jesus's power of attorney when you pray.

If you want to do business with the Father, don't try to come without the name of Jesus, because *His name is the key to heaven.* Jesus didn't say to list some good people's names to help your case when you pray. Why would anyone want their help when we have the Son? Martha, Mary, Luke, Philip, John, James, and the others were all faithful believers. Yet when Peter encountered the man at the gate Beautiful, he healed him in the name of Jesus, not in the name of the believers. He said, in effect, "I don't have any silver and gold. All I have is a name, *the* name, and I'm about to do business with heaven. The Father is working, and I see you healed already. Therefore, I am going to bring to earth what I see in heaven; but I have to do it through the legal channel." (See Acts 3:1–8.) No one but Jesus can be our legal channel to the Father.

We can appreciate the religious leaders in the world today and in history. However, Jesus said if we want to do business with the Father, we must come in His name alone. The Bible says, *"There is no other name under heaven given to men by which we must be saved"* (Acts 4:12). Our laws say that the person whose name is on the document as power of attorney is the only person who can legally give representation. According to God's Word, Jesus is the only one who can speak for you: *"For there is one God and one mediator between God and men, the man Christ Jesus"* (1 Timothy 2:5). The Scripture also says,

> *Therefore God exalted [Jesus] to the highest place and gave him the name that is above every name, that at the name of Jesus every knee should bow, in heaven and on earth and under the earth, and every tongue confess that Jesus Christ is Lord, to the glory of God the Father.* (Philippians 2:9–11)

Jesus's name is power in heaven, and every tongue will eventually confess that Jesus is Lord—Lord of everything. This truth is the basis on which we are to fulfill the Great Commission—telling others about the power of Jesus's name to save and deliver. (See Matthew 28:18–19.) Because he acted on Christ's authority, the apostle Paul, in addition to the other apostles, *"preached fearlessly in the name of Jesus"* (Acts 9:27). The courage and boldness we need to make disciples of all nations come from the authority we have been given in Jesus's name.

Thought: No one but Jesus can be our legal channel to the Father.

Reading: Matthew 28:18–19

CALL ON THE NAME

"To those sanctified in Christ Jesus and called to be holy, together with all those everywhere who call on the name of our Lord Jesus Christ—their Lord and ours."

—1 Corinthians 1:2

The Bible says, *"The name of the LORD is a strong tower; the righteous run to it and are safe"* (Proverbs 18:10). Perhaps you have been praying for something for a long time. Ask yourself today, "Have I prayed in the name of Jesus without thinking about what that name really means?" If you need healing, use the name of Jesus as you never have before, applying His name specifically to your situation. Perhaps you need deliverance from bad habits. To break those chains, you must use the power of His name.

There is no other name by which we should make our requests to God the Father but the name of Jesus. We must use what He has provided for us when we ask the Father to manifest His power in our lives and in the lives of others: the ability to make our requests based on God's nature and attributes, and the authority to pray in Jesus's name. Whenever you are in a difficult situation, instead of becoming fearful, anxious, or angry, run to the name of the Lord in prayer and call on Him as your Salvation and Righteousness and as your Protector and Defender.

"Some trust in chariots and some in horses, but we trust in the name of the LORD our God" (Psalm 20:7). Whatever you need, call on Him to fulfill that need based on who He is. Remember, since He is the I AM, His attributes are as numerous as your needs. He is Savior, Healer, Strengthener, Freedom, Joy, Wisdom, Kindness,

Friendship, Vision-Giver, Sustainer, Rent Payer, Business Grower, and so much more.

Call on the name of the Lord.

Let's pray together:

Heavenly Father,

As Psalm 8:1 says, *"How majestic is your name in all the earth!"* Your Word says that at the name of Jesus, every knee will bow and every tongue confess that Jesus is Lord over everything. Jesus said if we ask for anything in His name, You will do it. We know that we cannot ask in Jesus's name unless we ask what is according to Your will. However, we also know that when we ask in your Son's name, He will present our requests to You properly. He will pray in accordance with Your will. He will pray for us when we don't know what to say. He will appeal our case. So, Lord, we ask that Your will be done. There is no other name by which we make our requests but the name of Jesus. We call on the power of His name to meet all our needs. We pray in the name of Jesus, whose name is above all names. Amen!

Thought: Jesus's name is the *only* name that can activate power in heaven.

Reading: Psalm 8

THE POWER OF FASTING

"When you fast, put oil on your head and wash your face, so that it will not be obvious to men that you are fasting, but only to your Father, who is unseen; and your Father, who sees what is done in secret, will reward you." —Matthew 6:17–18

Prayer and fasting are equal parts of a single ministry. In Matthew 6:5–6, Jesus said, *"When you pray...."* He didn't say, "If you pray," but *"When you pray."* In the same passage, He said, *"When you fast...."* (verses 16, 17).

Just as prayer is not optional for the believer, fasting is not optional. It is a natural expectation of God for His people.[6] Christ is saying to us, "If you love Me, you will pray and fast." There are times when the Holy Spirit will move upon a person or group of people and supernaturally give them a desire to fast. Yet, the majority of the time, fasting is an act of our faith and our wills. It is a decision we make based on our love for Christ and our obedience to Him.

In the Old Testament, the Hebrew word for fast is *tsum*, which means "to cover over the mouth." In the New Testament, the Greek word is *nesteuo*, signifying "to abstain from food." A fast is a conscious, intentional decision to abstain for a time from the pleasure of eating *in order to gain vital spiritual benefits.*

All the greatest saints in the Bible fasted. Moses, David, Nehemiah, Jeremiah, Daniel, Anna, Paul, Peter, and even Jesus Himself fasted. Have you ever said to yourself anything like the following? "I wish I had the faith of Joshua, who made the sun

---

6. These are general biblical guidelines. If you have a medical condition or special health or medication concerns, use wisdom and consult your doctor before fasting.

stand still." "I wish I could be like Peter, whose shadow falling on people resulted in their healing." "I'd like to be like John, who received the Revelation from God." We admire these believers, but we don't often realize why such spiritual power was manifested in their lives. It was because they committed themselves to high standards in the practice of their faith so that God could use them to fulfill His purposes. Prayer and fasting were a normal part of their lives.

Fasting is one of the pillars of the Christian faith. It is mentioned in Scripture one-third as much as prayer. Yet most Christians put fasting in the background of their experience as believers. Many consider the regular practice of fasting to be almost fanatical.

While fasting used to be seen as valuable and significant in the Christian church, it has become a lost art. So little is taught and practiced in regard to fasting that it is not understood by most believers, especially young Christians who are just coming into the body of Christ. They don't hear about or see any older believers fasting, so they conclude that it is something that has only historical significance. For this reason, in the next several devotions, I want to give you some guidelines to help you understand what fasting is and why God says we are to fast.

As we move forward with this topic, here is a key point to understand: *fasting should be a natural part of the life of a believer.* In the same way that we practice the habits of reading the Bible and praying, we should practice the habit of fasting.

⌐⌐

Thought: Fasting is one of the pillars of the Christian faith.

Reading: Luke 5:33–35

—— DAY 84 ——

THE PURPOSE OF FASTING

"I proclaimed a fast, so that we might humble ourselves before our God and ask him for a safe journey for us and our children, with all our possessions."
                                                            —Ezra 8:21

What is the purpose of fasting? True fasting involves these characteristics:

Seeking God. First, fasting is a time set apart to seek the face of God. It means abstaining from other things that you find pleasure in for the purpose of giving your whole heart to God in prayer. When you fast, you're telling God, "My prayer and the answers I'm seeking are more important than my pleasure in eating."

Putting God first. Second, fasting means putting God first, focusing all your attention on Him alone—not on His gifts or blessings, but on God Himself. It shows God how much you love and appreciate Him, that you want Him more than you do your business or your busy-ness. In this way, fasting is a point of intimacy with God. God will reveal Himself only to people who want to know Him. He says, *"You will seek me and find me when you seek me with all your heart"* (Jeremiah 29:13).

Thus, fasting signifies that God alone is who you want. You don't want what He has to give you; you want *Him.* It's not a matter of your trying to get something from God. It's a matter of your trying to get *to* God. That's because, when you find God Himself, you will discover that everything you need comes with Him.

Creating an environment for prayer. Third, fasting is a time to foster a sensitive environment for the working of prayer. Almost always, when you read about fasting in the Bible, it has the word *prayer* coupled with it. In the Old Testament, people fasted in conjunction with wholehearted prayer in times of mourning and repentance. Fasting was also used as a point of deliverance from various situations. Often, when an enemy army was challenging the people of God, the Israelites would commit themselves to several days of fasting. They would say, in effect, "We will fast until the Lord tells us what to do." The Lord would respond and give them a strategy, and they would win the battle. Therefore, fasting helps to create the environment for God to work. It enables us to see the fulfillment of God's Word and purposes for us as individuals and as members of the body of Christ.

Interceding for others. Fourth, fasting is a form of intercession for others. In the majority of cases in the Bible, when any person or people fasted, it was on behalf of the needs of others, whether it was a national problem or a family situation. People fasted to bring God into their circumstances. (See, for example, Esther 4:15–16; Daniel 10:1–3; Nehemiah 1; 2 Chronicles 20:1–4.) I believe those who fast benefit from their obedience in fasting. However, the main purpose of fasting is to benefit others. Fasting goes beyond just praying because sometimes our prayers can be selfish. Fasting takes prayer into a completely different realm.

⌣

Thought: Fasting enables us to see the fulfillment of God's Word and purposes for us as individuals and as members of the body of Christ.

Reading: 2 Chronicles 20:1–18

— Day 85 —

ATTAINING GUIDANCE, WISDOM, INSTRUCTION, AND KNOWLEDGE

"Moses was there with the LORD forty days and forty nights without eating bread or drinking water." —Exodus 34:28

We need to understand the value and significance of emptying ourselves of food and filling ourselves with God. Fasting enables us to increase our spiritual capacity. It exerts discipline over our physical appetites. It brings the body under subjection to what the spirit desires. We are spirits, but we live in bodies. Most of the time, our bodies control us. When you fast, your spirit increases its control over your body. Fasting enables you to discipline your body so that the body becomes a servant of the Lord, rather than the master of your spirit. Your body begins to obey your spirit rather than its own impulses and habits.

Fasting does not change God; *it changes us*, and it transforms our prayers. We don't realize the power that flows through fasting. In the next few devotions, we will explore several powerful results of fasting.

First, fasting allows us to attain guidance, wisdom, instruction, and knowledge from God. When Moses went up on Mount Sinai, he was seeking God's will for the Israelite people, and God took him on a forty-day fast. *"Moses was there with the LORD forty days and forty nights without eating bread or drinking water"* (Exodus 34:28).

At the end of this fast, the Lord gave Moses a powerful revelation—the Law, with its Ten Commandments—which many nations have used as the foundation of their societies. All of our penal codes are based on the Law that Moses received during his forty-day fast. That's how powerful that fast was. When you fast, God is going to speak to you. You are going to receive a revelation from Him that you couldn't receive otherwise.

In the early church, the leaders spent time fasting and praying to hear from God before making decisions and when commissioning believers for ministry. Acts 13:2 says, *"While they were worshiping the Lord and fasting, the Holy Spirit said, 'Set apart for me Barnabas and Saul [Paul] for the work to which I have called them.' So after they had fasted and prayed, they placed their hands on them and sent them off."* While traveling in their God-given ministry, Paul and Barnabas did the same: *"Paul and Barnabas appointed elders for them in each church and, with prayer and fasting, committed them to the Lord, in whom they had put their trust"* (Acts 14:23).

When you are fasting, the time you would have spent on meals should be spent in prayer and Bible study so that you can hear what God wants to say to you. It's amazing how many hours a day we normally spend on food. Planning meals, shopping, cooking, eating, and cleaning up are very time-consuming. When you fast, all that time becomes available for you to seek God. God has always desired a close relationship with you, and during a fast, there is time for true intimacy to begin to develop.

Thought: Fasting does not change God; it changes us, and it transforms our prayers.

Reading: Daniel 10:1–21

— DAY 86 —

RECEIVING THE FULLNESS OF
GOD'S POWER

"Jesus returned to Galilee in the power of the Spirit."
—Luke 4:14

A *second powerful result of fasting is that it enables us to receive the fullness of God's power for ministry.* Sometimes prayer alone is not enough to accomplish God's purposes. The Bible records the account of a man whose son was demon-possessed, and Jesus's disciples were trying to cast out the demon, but the demon was laughing at them. Why? They were not prepared. Then Jesus came and cast out the demon. The disciples pulled Jesus aside and asked why they hadn't been able to do this. His answer was, *"This kind does not go out except by prayer and fasting"* (Matthew 17:21 NKJV).

Christ was able to cast out any demon He was confronted with because He had spent forty days preparing Himself for ministry through prayer and fasting, and because He continued to pray and fast on a regular basis. When Jesus told His disciples that the demon who was afflicting the man's son could come out only by prayer and fasting, He was saying, in effect, "You have prayed for this man's son to be delivered, and prayer is good. However, sometimes you need to add something to your prayers: a spirit of consecration to God and an abstinence from what can interfere with the flow of God's power in your life."

When Jesus was on earth, He had the full capacity of God's anointing to meet the needs of the people. Yet fasting was still a necessity for Him. The Bible says, *"Jesus, full of the Holy Spirit, returned from the Jordan and was led by the Spirit in the desert, where for forty days he was tempted by the devil. He ate nothing during those* days" (Luke 4:1–2). Then it says, *"When the devil had finished all this tempting, he left him until an opportune time. Jesus returned to Galilee* **in the power of the Spirit***"* (Luke 4:13–14).

Forty days earlier, when Jesus had been baptized by John in the Jordan, the heavens had opened, and the Holy Spirit had come upon Him. (See Luke 3:21–22.) Yet, we read that, after He fasted, He returned *"in the power of the Spirit"*—whom He had already received before the fast. Jesus didn't receive the Holy Spirit after He fasted, but the Spirit within Him was manifested with *new power* after His fast.

Similarly, although you received the Holy Spirit when you were born again, a fast will ignite His power within you. When you fast, you will develop a hunger for God as well as an intimacy with Him, and the work of the Holy Spirit will be powerfully manifested in your life. Your love for the Father will be renewed. It will be a joy for you to witness to others about God's love and grace. You will be able to serve God in ways you never expected. Fasting will prepare you for ministry.

⌣

Thought: Fasting enables us to receive the fullness of God's power for ministry.

Prayer: John 3:34

EXPERIENCING BREAKTHROUGHS IN DIFFICULT SITUATIONS

"Be not afraid, O land; be glad and rejoice. Surely the Lord has done great things."　　　　　　　　　　—Joel 2:21

A third result of fasting is that it often brings breakthroughs in difficult circumstances or in the lives of those who are resistant to the gospel. In the first chapter of Joel, we read,

> *The vine is dried up and the fig tree is withered; the pomegranate, the palm and the apple tree—all the trees of the field—are dried up.... Come, spend the night in sackcloth, you who minister before my God; for the grain offerings and drink offerings are withheld from the house of your God.* **Declare a holy fast;** *call a sacred assembly. Summon the elders and all who live in the land to the house of the Lord your God, and cry out to the Lord.*　　　　　　　　　　(Joel 1:12–14)

This seems like a very depressing passage of Scripture, doesn't it? It talks about all the things that are lacking. Everything had gone wrong, and nothing was working for the Israelites. However, the Lord had the answer. He said, *"Declare a holy fast."* Likewise, when things are tough, when you aren't experiencing a breakthrough, or nothing seems to be happening in your life, God says, "Stop everything and consecrate yourself. Come to Me."

In Joel 2:18–32, the Lord said, in essence, "After you fast, get ready, because something good is going to happen!" Let's look at a portion of that passage:

> *Be not afraid, O land; be glad and rejoice. Surely the Lord has done great things.... The trees are bearing their fruit; the*

fig tree and the vine yield their riches.... He sends you abun-
dant showers, both autumn and spring rains, as before. The
threshing floors will be filled with grain; the vats will overflow
with new wine and oil.   (Joel 2:21–24)

The result of sincere fasting and prayer is that God responds, bringing deliverance and blessing.

Have you been praying and believing God about some things for a long time? You probably need to add fasting to your prayers. I used to wonder why my mother would say to my brothers and sisters and me, "All of you are going to get saved. I'm fasting for you all." My mother would often go on fasts. She would say about one of her sons, "He's running off and getting into trouble. I have to go on a fast." She used to call it "paying the price for him." My mother saw all of her eleven children saved before she went to be with the Lord. Praying isn't enough for some children. They're so tough that you have to go a little deeper through fasting in order for them to be delivered.

Perhaps you have been trusting God for years to bring certain family members, friends, and acquaintances to Christ. It is possible that the evil spirits from the enemy who are deceiving them aren't going to leave unless you add fasting to your prayers. Or perhaps you have been praying for a breakthrough at your workplace. You can fast for that situation, also. When you "pay the price" by praying and fasting, God will respond.

⌒

Thought: The result of sincere fasting and prayer is that God responds, bringing deliverance and blessing.

Reading: Joel 2:12–13

THE RIGHT WAY TO FAST

"Is not this the kind of fasting I have chosen: to loose the chains
of injustice and untie the cords of the yoke, to set the oppressed
free and break every yoke?" —Isaiah 58:6

When we consecrate ourselves in fasting, we need to be careful not to hinder the effectiveness of our fast. Fasting must be done in the right spirit. Isaiah 58 tells us right and wrong ways to fast. In verse three, God quoted the Israelites: *"'Why have we fasted,' they say, 'and you have not seen it? Why have we humbled ourselves, and you have not noticed?'"* God's reply was,

> *Yet on the day of your fasting, you do as you please and exploit*
> *all your workers. Your fasting ends in quarreling and strife,*
> *and in striking each other with wicked fists. You cannot fast as*
> *you do today and expect your voice to be heard on high.*
>
> (verses 3–4)

What was the problem with the Israelites' fasting? It was characterized by injustice to others and ended in *"quarreling and strife."* When God says, *"Declare a holy fast; call a sacred assembly"* (Joel 1:14), He is saying, "Call people away from their regular duties and have them fast as a holy duty to Me." If we *"do as we please"* when we fast, instead of seeking and obeying God, He will say to us, "Do you expect Me to answer your prayers while you have this attitude?"

Fasting is no game. God wants us to earnestly seek Him and His ways. In turn, He will pour out His power through us.

Is not this the kind of fasting I have chosen: to loose the chains
of injustice and untie the cords of the yoke, to set the oppressed

free and break every yoke? Is it not to share your food with the hungry and to provide the poor wanderer with shelter—when you see the naked, to clothe him, and not to turn away from your own flesh and blood? Then your light will break forth like the dawn, and your healing will quickly appear; then your righteousness will go before you, and the glory of the LORD will be your rear guard. (Isaiah 58:6–8)

Isaiah says that the fast God is pleased with has the power to break the chains of injustice and destroy the yokes of the oppressed. God's anointing can deliver people from their burdens. This anointing comes through fasting that is consecrated and committed to God. Therefore, a true fast will cause you to understand and value the important things in life. You will become a giver. You will begin to love people and want to meet their needs. You will have a burden for souls. People's lives will be restored to God (see Isaiah 58:12), and you will also receive God's blessings. *"Then your light will break forth like the dawn, and your healing will quickly appear"* (Isaiah 58:8). You have an opportunity to activate your faith for healing when you fast. The same verse says, *"Your righteousness will go before you, and the glory of the LORD will be your rear guard."* The Lord will protect you. These are just some of the blessings that come as a result of a fast that is pleasing to God.

⌒

Thought: Our fasting must be done in the right spirit.

Reading: Matthew 6:16–18

— Day 89 —
GET READY TO BE FILLED

"Then you will call, and the LORD will answer; you will cry for help, and he will say: Here am I." —Isaiah 58:9

When you fast, you're setting yourself up for answered prayer. God has promised that if you fast in the right way, He will hear and answer. *"Then you will call, and the LORD will answer; you will cry for help, and he will say: Here am I"* (Isaiah 58:9). When you fast, you are open to God. Your spiritual capacity to hear and receive is increased. You are empty of your own interests, and you are ready for Him to fill you.

Remember, God *expects* His people to fast; it is not optional.[7] In the same way we practice the habits of Bible reading and prayer, we should practice the habit of fasting. Let's review some of the major points about fasting:

+ Fasting is a time set apart to seek the face of God and to abstain from other things in order to give one's whole heart to the Lord in prayer.

+ Fasting means putting God first, focusing all of one's attention on Him alone.

+ Fasting is a time to foster a sensitive environment for the working of prayer.

+ Fasting is a form of intercession for others.

+ Fasting does not change God; it changes *us* and our prayers.

+ Fasting allows us to receive guidance, wisdom, instruction, and knowledge from God.

---

7. Again, if you have a medical condition or special health or medication concerns, use wisdom and consult your doctor before fasting.

- Fasting enables us to receive the fullness of the Spirit for ministry.
- Fasting brings breakthroughs in difficult circumstances and in the lives of those who are resistant to the gospel.

We need to keep in mind that there is a right way and a wrong way to fast. The right way is to be consecrated and committed to God, maintain the right priorities, lift people's burdens, have the heart of a giver, show love to others, and have a burden for souls. The wrong way is to treat others with injustice, quarrel and cause strife, and pursue our own pleasures rather than God's will.

In a true fast, we can expect people to be delivered and restored to God. The one who fasts receives God's blessings as well. Begin to add fasting to your prayer life. To make fasting a true spiritual habit, you may want to start with one meal or one day a week and gradually increase the time you fast.

Let's pray together:

Heavenly Father,

You have taught us that when we pray, we are to bring others' needs with us. Fasting is a form of intercession, and we want to be empowered by Your Spirit through fasting so we can minister to others and counteract the work of the enemy. We consecrate ourselves to You in prayer and fasting, setting ourselves apart to seek You and Your will rather than our own interests. Use us to fulfill Your purposes for Your glory. We pray this in the name of Jesus, amen.

Thought: Fasting is a time set apart to seek the face of God and to abstain from other things in order to give one's whole heart to God in prayer.

Reading: Psalm 27:8

BECOME A PERSON OF PRAYER

"Be joyful always; pray continually; give thanks in all circumstances, for this is God's will for you in Christ Jesus."
—1 Thessalonians 5:16–17

One thing the Lord has made clear through His Word is that prayer is not optional. It is a necessity!

During these days together, we have explored many powerful principles of prayer. Prayer is our invitation to God to intervene in the affairs of earth, our agreement with His sovereign will, and our request for Him to work His ways in this world. It is a vital part of God's purpose in creation—and it is something we are called to pursue.

I would like to challenge you to take the principles presented in this devotional and test them. Begin praying according to the Word of God and in the name of Jesus. Discover your power, your authority, and your rights as an intercessor for the earth. In short, *become a person of prayer.*

A person of prayer...

+ recognizes that prayer is a sacred trust from God.

+ understands their purpose in life as God's priest and intercessor for the world.

+ has a relationship of trust with the heavenly Father and desires the world to experience the power of His presence and life.

+ knows that the will of God will flow forth from heaven to earth only through their prayers and the prayers of all God's people.

If we understand God's plan for prayer yet fail to pursue it, we are like the person who sees their reflection in the mirror but then immediately forgets what they look like. (See James 1:22–25.) The absolute necessity of prayer must be like an indelible image upon our hearts and minds. If we want to see God's will done on earth, we must do our part—we must *pray*.

God desires for you to partner with Him in the great purpose of reclaiming and redeeming the world. The Scripture says, *"If my people, who are called by my name, will humble themselves and pray and seek my face and turn from their wicked ways, then will I hear from heaven and will forgive their sin and will heal their land"* (2 Chronicles 7:14). God is saying, *"If my people,…then will I."* Once again, God has called His people to be His priests or intercessors. This refers to the *entire* body of Christ, not just an elite group of "intercessory prayer warriors" in the local church. All of us have the power to bring God's will on earth so the world can be healed and transformed by His grace.

Remember, God's will on earth can be executed only through the cooperation of mankind. Prayer is this medium of cooperation. Prayer is therefore the most important activity of humanity.

The earth is depending on you to pray. The families of the earth are depending on you to pray. Your children's children are depending on you to pray. All creation is depending on you to pray. Heaven is depending on you to pray. I challenge you to fulfill your obligation to your generation and to the future of planet earth: *pray.*

⌣⌐

Thought: Prayer is the most important activity of humanity.

Reading: Revelation 11:15

ABOUT THE AUTHOR

D r. Myles Munroe (1954–2014) was an international motivational speaker, best-selling author, educator, leadership mentor, and consultant for government and business. Traveling extensively throughout the world, Dr. Munroe addressed critical issues affecting the full range of human, social, and spiritual development. He was a popular author of more than forty books, including *Understanding the Purpose and Power of Prayer, The Principles and Power of Vision, The Power of Character in Leadership, The Spirit of Leadership,* and the devotionals *A Woman of Purpose and Power, A Man of Purpose and Power,* and *Vision with Purpose and Power.*

Dr. Munroe was the founder and president of Bahamas Faith Ministries International (BFMI), a multidimensional organization headquartered in Nassau, Bahamas. He was the chief executive officer and chairman of the board of the International Third World Leaders Association and president of the International Leadership Training Institute.

Dr. Munroe earned B.A. and M.A. degrees from Oral Roberts University and the University of Tulsa, and was awarded a number of honorary doctoral degrees. The parents of two adult children, Charisa and Chairo (Myles Jr.), Dr. Munroe and his wife, Ruth, traveled as a team and were involved in teaching seminars together. Both were leaders who ministered with sensitive hearts and international vision. In November 2014, they were tragically killed in an airplane crash en route to an annual leadership conference sponsored by Bahamas Faith Ministries International. A statement from Dr. Munroe in his book *The Power of Character in Leadership* summarizes his own legacy: "Remember that character ensures the longevity of leadership, and men and women of principle will leave important legacies and be remembered by future generations."